The **PocketScroll**® Series

# HARMONY

*with*

A PocketScroll® Book

# RABBI ZELIG PLISKIN

# OTHERS

## Formulas, stories and insights

# HARMONY WITH OTHERS:
## PREVENTING AND RESOLVING QUARRELS

| | | |
|---|---|---|
| | Introduction | 9 |
| 1. | Love Peace and Pursue Peace | 13 |
| 2. | What Is Peace? What Is Lack of Peace? | 15 |
| 3. | Enjoyable Times | 17 |
| 4. | The Greeting of Peace | 19 |
| 5. | What's Really Important in Your Life? | 21 |
| 6. | Solutions Versus Blaming | 23 |
| 7. | "What's The Best Option for Dealing With This?" | 26 |
| 8. | Be Concise and Focus on Your Outcome | 29 |
| 9. | King Solomon's Wise Formula | 32 |
| 10. | Who Is an Honorable Person? | 34 |
| 11. | My Partner in Personal Growth | 36 |
| 12. | From the Perspective of Our Father, Our King | 38 |
| 13. | Pray for Peace | 40 |
| 14. | "How Did I Contribute?" | 42 |
| 15. | The Drama of Quarrels | 44 |

| | | |
|---|---|---|
| 16. | Aaron's Strategy | 46 |
| 17. | The Most Common Mistake of Outsiders | 48 |
| 18. | Your Self-Image Creates You | 51 |
| 19. | Self-Image Might Cause Unawareness | 54 |
| 20. | Tone of Voice | 56 |
| 21. | Tone Down Rhetoric | 59 |
| 22. | Communication as a Loop | 61 |
| 23. | Inner Calm for Harmony with Others | 64 |
| 24. | Win-Win Approach | 67 |
| 25. | Agreement Frame | 69 |
| 26. | Learn From Your Strengths and Successes | 72 |
| 27. | Understanding Even if You Don't Agree | 75 |
| 28. | Mental Rehearsals | 77 |
| 29. | Twelve Powerful Words | 79 |
| 30. | Repeating Your Apology | 81 |
| 31. | "They" Should Start | 83 |
| 32. | We Can Only Be in the Present | 85 |
| 33. | When It's Over, Let It Remain Over | 88 |
| 34. | "I Wish I Could Redo That." | 90 |
| 35. | If It Doesn't Work, Do Something Else | 92 |
| 36. | Learn From the Successes of Others | 95 |
| 37. | Patience and Persistence | 97 |
| 38. | Let the Other Person Express His Feelings | 99 |
| 39. | What Are the Real Issues? | 102 |
| 40. | Stay on Track | 105 |
| 41. | Small Steps at a Time | 107 |
| 42. | Setbacks Are Part of the Process | 109 |

| | | |
|---|---|---|
| 43. | Levels of Apologies | 111 |
| 44. | Forgive! | 113 |
| 45. | Keep Entering the Other Person's Mind | 115 |
| 46. | The Greatness of Going Against Your Feelings | 117 |
| 47. | Act as if in a Play | 119 |
| 48. | Expect People to Think Differently | 122 |
| 49. | Know That You Don't Know | 125 |
| 50. | Stating What You Really Feel | 128 |
| 51. | Seeing The Pain of the Other | 130 |
| 52. | It's Just a Test | 132 |
| 53. | Facial Expressions | 134 |
| 54. | Respect Each Person's Potential | 136 |
| 55. | What Do You Both Really Want? | 138 |
| 56. | Change, Rather Than Hide, Negative Feelings | 140 |
| 57. | Timing Is Crucial | 142 |
| 58. | If You Knew You Would Succeed | 144 |
| 59. | If It Won't Help, Don't Start an Avoidable Quarrel | 146 |
| 60. | Find Humor in Things that Used to Get You Upset | 148 |
| 61. | Defensive or Aggressive? | 150 |
| 62. | "What Would Happen If...?" | 152 |
| 63. | "If I Can Show You a Better Way...?" | 154 |
| 64. | Your Thoughts Are Energy | 157 |
| 65. | Mistaken Assumptions | 159 |
| 66. | Transcending Insults | 162 |
| 67. | What Do You Choose to Overlook? | 166 |

| | | |
|---|---|---|
| 68. | It's the Principle | 168 |
| 69. | If I Give In, He Will Feel that He Was Totally Right | 170 |
| 70. | Financial Disputes | 172 |
| 71. | Impulsivity | 174 |
| 72. | The Memory of the Written Word | 176 |
| 73. | Mocking Remarks | 178 |
| 74. | Self-Deception About One's Motives | 181 |
| 75. | Being Right, Dead Right | 183 |
| 76. | Misrepresenting Your Position | 185 |
| 77. | "Just Do It My Way" | 187 |
| 78. | Don't Be Bullied Mentally | 190 |
| 79. | Skeptics, Cynics, and Sarcasm | 193 |
| 80. | Charming in Front of Others | 196 |
| 81. | Don't Fall Into a Naïve Trap | 199 |
| 82. | Don't Make Things Worse | 201 |
| 83. | Withstanding Negative Approaches of Others | 203 |
| 84. | Don't Judge Others | 206 |
| 85. | Find an Objective Mediator | 208 |
| 86. | "He Agreed with Me." | 210 |
| 87. | Time Release Suggestions | 213 |
| 88. | Can Nothing Be Done? | 215 |
| 89. | Know Your Limitations | 218 |
| 90. | At Times Only Distance Will Prevent Quarrels | 221 |
| 91. | Peace at any Cost Can Be too Expensive | 223 |
| 92. | Time Is Running Out | 225 |
| 93. | Believe In Miracles | 227 |

# INTRODUCTION

PEACE IS SUCH A BEAUTIFUL CONCEPT. WE CONSTANTLY pray for peace. Many poetic words have been written to express profound thoughts and feelings about the value of peace.

About the opposite of peace, it's often been said, "War is Hell." Not the most pleasant of expressions to start off a book. But the reality of lack of peace is much worse, not only militarily, but within families or between friends, neighbors, colleagues, and complete strangers. The emotional harm can be deep and long-lasting.

In theory we all want peace, and in practice we all need peace. And if one isn't involved in a specific argument, quarrel, or fight, one will readily say, "Everyone should make peace."

But the reality is that it's so easy not to have peace. People say things we don't like. People do things we don't like. People don't do the things that we would want them to do. Of course if everyone would always be exactly the way we wanted them to be, we would always have peace. So it's always the other person's fault if there isn't peace, isn't that so? No, it isn't always so. Because from the other person's perspective, any lack of peace is our fault. We are the ones who caused lack of peace and if we would change, then there would be peace.

Lack of peace can truly be caused by circumstances completely beyond our control. Still, there is much we can do to prevent quarrels in the first place, and to resolve problematic situations that do arise.

Many issues are discussed in this book: What are the attitudes that will help us be more peaceful? What patterns of communication are conducive to peace? What can we say and do to resolve quarrels? What are patterns that we should avoid? What can we say and do to help other people make peace?

Mastering the ability to be patient and serene is conducive to peace. In two previous books in this ArtScroll series, *Patience* and *Serenity*, we have elaborated on how to integrate these qualities. When you experience these states, you will find it much easier to speak and act in ways that are conducive to peace. And if someone finds that the state of anger is a root cause of their quarrels, the nine step program found in *Anger: The Inner Teacher* (ArtScroll) is highly recommended.

Some situations are simple to resolve, but it's not always so easy to do and say what would be effective. It can take much inner strength and courage to say what we all know would be best to say. Other situations are highly complex. Short aphorisms and clichés and simplistic suggestions totally miss the point. It takes the wisdom of the wisest of people to understand the inner workings of the minds of all parties involved and to come up with highly creative solutions that will satisfy everyone's needs.

Realizing our helplessness, we can humbly call upon our Father, our King, Creator and Sustainer of the universe, to create a spirit of peace in this world. May the Almighty give each of us the wisdom to say what needs to be said for peace.

If this book were to be read by everyone who could read and followed by all, the author would probably receive the Nobel Peace Prize. Since the author tries to be realistic, he knows that this isn't very likely. But if some readers will actually benefit, the efforts were greatly worthwhile. And since you are reading this now, may this refer to you.

As with the other books in this series, the stories are the experiences of many different people. All information that could identify any individual has been deleted. The stories are presented in the first person, describing situations from the point of view of those who experienced them.

I wish to express my profound gratitude to Hashem for giving me life and for making this book possible. May our prayers for peace be answered and may the entire world experience true and everlasting peace.

I thank Rabbi Meir Zlotowitz, Rabbi Shmuel Blitz, Rabbi Avrohom Biderman, and the entire ArtScroll staff for their efforts to transform this book from a manuscript to a published book.

I am grateful to Rabbi Noah Weinberg, founder and head of Aish HaTorah, for his idealism and intense drive to spread the fire of Torah.

Thank you, Rabbi Kalman Packouz, for your continued friendship and encouragement.

I am deeply grateful to my brother-in-law, Rabbi Hershel Weizberg, for his ongoing kindness and patience. May Hashem bless him in all ways.

For those who wish to gain greater mastery over the states and traits that are conducive to peace, I would recommend listening to my recorded seminar, "Creating the states you want: more joy, less distress." TM

# 1

# LOVE PEACE
# AND PURSUE PEACE

THE GREAT SAGE HILLEL TELLS US, "BE A STUDENT OF AARON: Love peace and pursue peace" (*Pirkei Avos* 1:11).

When you love someone or something, the object of your love is a high priority for you. In the Torah we read how Jacob was willing to work seven full years in order to marry Rachel whom he loved. The Torah tells us that these seven years were considered as just a few days in his eyes. Imagine loving peace to the same extent.

When you've integrated a love of peace, you will be willing to put in much energy and effort to attain it. You might have to make sacrifices, which come in many forms. When love is a motivating factor, you are more likely to make the necessary sacrifices.

"Pursue peace." You might have to take the initiative to approach people to make peace. Peace is likely to run away, as it were. How far are you willing to go for the sake of peace? The degree is likely to be commensurate with your love of peace.

There are always multiple perspectives to any situation. There are many ways to view what people say and do. A perspective of judging favorably is conducive to peace. And a love of peace frame will motivate you to prevent and resolve quarrels even in challenging situations.

How do you build up a love of peace? The same way you build up positive feelings towards another person: You focus on virtues. The more virtues you see in someone, the more positively you will feel towards him. Reflect on the benefits and virtues of peace.

A question to keep in mind is: "If I had an intense love of peace, what would I be willing to say and do?"

*"I've always felt that peace was important, and I was careful not to say negative things to others. But if someone hurt my feelings, I would keep a distance from that person, and would avoid doing any favors for him," someone shared with me when I told him that I was writing a book about peace.*

*"If you would sincerely love and pursue peace, in what ways would you act differently than you are now?" I asked him.*

*"I have to think about it," he replied.*

*"Great! Thinking about ideas is exactly what we need to internalize the essence of the ideas."*

*A week later he told me that he realized that he liked peace, but didn't really love it. He was motivated now to upgrade his like to love, and he had taken some constructive action in that direction.*

# 2

# WHAT IS PEACE?
# WHAT IS LACK OF PEACE?

PEACE HAS MANY LEVELS AND MANY DEFINITIONS. WHAT would be considered peace in certain situations might be considered lack of peace in other situations. And what would be considered lack of peace for certain people, might be considered peace for others.

On one level, peace is when two people or two sides interact together with a total sense of harmony and unity. At the opposite side, peace might be when two people or parties who were actively engaged in hostile and aggressive interactions now treat each other civilly and politely. They wouldn't want to spend an excessive amount of time together, but they are at peace in light of their previous relationship.

There could be situations when one person would say, "We now have peace," but the other would say, "We are far from real peace." If both are open to understanding the other's thoughts on the matter, they might be able to improve the situation.

People who get into bitter quarrels and feuds might attain a level of peace by minimizing their time together, and by avoiding the types of discussions that are just a source of distress.

On the other hand, there are people who could improve their relationship by discussing their disagreements. At first the intense emotions on both sides might seem like an all-out verbal battle. But by expressing themselves and listening to what the other has to say, they will be able to settle their dispute. For them, their heated discussion is a step forward towards peace.

*Someone who viewed peace as people interacting harmoniously and smoothly spent a week with a family that argued a lot. To this person's surprise, one of the family members happened to mention that their family gets along remarkably well. He was about to argue and say, "You argue way too much." He caught himself and realized that although he felt there was too much stress in this family, they were so used to expressing themselves emphatically that they didn't consider their arguments to be quarrels. What would have been distressful to him was considered totally acceptable to them.*

# 3
# ENJOYABLE TIMES

QUARRELS AND ANGRY EXCHANGES HAVE THE power to mess up enjoyable times. Celebrations and festivals are marred by lack of peace. Vacations can be spoiled, even ruined, by arguments over petty and inconsequential details. Shouting matches replace happiness, enjoyment, and relaxation with negative energy.

Peace is a prerequisite for enjoying celebrations, festivals, and vacations. The more special the occasion, the greater the damage caused by lack of peace.

During enjoyable times, you will have to answer the following question for yourself: "Is it worthwhile to choose words and actions that will create distress right now?" Put in this form, we will often see clearly that we would be wise to refrain from words and actions that will cause or prolong an unpleasant argument or quarrel.

Even on a regular, average day we will have much to appreciate and for which to be grateful. We can make enjoyable times our standard state. And since we have this choice, isn't it wiser to do what we can to sustain the positive instead of choosing words and actions that will create negativity? You can create an inner message: "Choose words and actions of peace and harmony and make the most of your present moments."

*"I used to have a terrible temper," the middle-aged family man shared with me. "Sabbath meals, holidays, and even bar-mitzvahs and weddings were a source of pain. In hindsight it became clear to me that my temper would flare up more when I wasn't running my business and trying to be polite to my customers. I used to blame other people for my self-caused misery. Family members made mistakes they should have known not to make. Waiters were slow and inefficient. There were always things to complain about and my angry kvetching often created arguments and quarrels. A few years ago, my physician told me, 'Either you will learn to take it easy or your heart won't last long enough for you to attend many more celebrations.' That was a shock to me. But a healthy one, for I became totally committed to remaining calm. I still have pain when I realize how much I ruined potentially great times. This increases my resolve to focus on what's really important."*

# 4
# THE GREETING OF PEACE

THE HEBREW WORD FOR PEACE IS *SHALOM*. WE GREET people with *shalom* when we encounter them. And we bless people with *shalom* when we say goodbye. When seeing someone for the first time, or when seeing someone we haven't seen in a long time, we use the traditional greeting of *"Shalom Aleichem,"* which means "peace unto you."

The word *shalom* means both peace and harmony. It has the same root as *sholaim,* which means wholeness. When there is an atmosphere of harmony, we feel whole and complete. And when a person feels whole, he is more likely to be at peace with himself and with others.

We bless people with peace. They should have inner peace and peace with others. When you have harmony, you function at your best. When two people work in harmony, they bring out the best in each other. When there is harmony in an organization or a community, everyone brings out the best in everyone else. And we are all very different at our best than we are at our worst.

Every time you say or hear the greeting of *"shalom"* you have a reminder of the importance and value of peace. Let each greeting remind you to be careful not to say things that create the opposite of peace. And just as people greet each other with blessings of peace, because we want others to have harmony in their lives, so, too, we should think about what we can say and do to bring peace among those who lack it.

*I knew someone who wasn't on very good terms with a colleague of his. I hadn't seen them in a while and when I met them at a wedding of a mutual acquaintance, I saw them sitting at the same table, engaged in friendly conversation. I told the person I knew, "I'm interested in the process of people improving their interactions. Is there anything in your experience that I can learn from?"*

*He said, "I was ill for about two weeks. When I returned to work, my colleague greeted me with an amazing smile, one of the friendliest greetings of Shalom Aleichem that I have ever heard, and said to me, 'I'm so glad that you are well.' This expression of positive feelings about my recovery enabled me to focus on his good qualities and on what I respect and like about him."*

THINK BEFORE YOU
        SPEAK!

# 5

# WHAT'S REALLY
# IMPORTANT
# IN YOUR LIFE?

WE ALL ARE PRONE TO HAVE CONFLICTS OF INTEREST with others. Even the youngest of children will quarrel over toys, over the largest portion of ice cream, over who gets to sit where. Even though the young children might quarrel passionately, adults look at these quarrels and view them as <u>trivial and petty</u>.

The most important questions each of us needs to answer are, "What are you living for? What is the purpose of your life?" And this brings us to the question, "<u>What's really important in your life?</u>" From this viewpoint, most quarrels are over trivial matters. From a mature, eternal perspective, the quarrels of many adults are not that far from the quarrels of two young children over a small toy.

When you are aware of what is really important in your life, you will be much calmer when you discuss and negotiate conflicts of interest. Trivial matters are seen as trivial. Solutions still need to be found, but you will find it easier to maintain your composure. Your peaceful patterns will influence the other person to be more peaceful also. 

When we look back at arguments and quarrels fought a number of years ago, we see them much differently than we did when we first experienced them. In hindsight we have a greater sense of perspective. The more life experience we have, the greater our awareness of the loss and harm of quarrels and the benefits of peaceful interactions.

So before getting involved in a quarrel, ask yourself:

"Compared to my ultimate purpose in life, how important is this?"

"From the perspective of eternity, is it worth spending my time now on this quarrel?"

"How can I refine my character while I search for a mutually acceptable solution?"

"Will I regret that I did not quarrel now when I eventually look back at my entire life?"

*When I was a young student, a rabbi of mine passed by when I was involved in an angry quarrel with another student. He said to us with a smile, "You are both too valuable to spend your time in a petty quarrel. Think of all the potential uses of time right now that you can choose. In the future, how would you have wished to have spent your time?"*

*Understandably, we both stopped fighting. I have often avoided quarrels by remembering what he told us. The quarrel was over something trivial, but the lesson we learned was invaluable.*

# 6

# SOLUTIONS
# VERSUS BLAMING

WHEN YOU FIND YOURSELF IN A CONFLICT WITH someone, focus on finding solutions. This is in contrast to thinking and speaking in terms of blaming.

Some blaming patterns are:

"It's your fault that we are fighting."

"If you were more reasonable, we wouldn't argue so much."

"Your negative character traits are at the root of all our problems in getting along."

"If you were different, we would get along just fine."

"Any objective outsider would agree that you are totally wrong and I am totally right."

The person on the receiving end of this blaming rarely responds:

"You're right. It's all my fault. I'll act better from now on."

"Yes. I need to take a course to learn how to be more reasonable. When I master Reasonableness 101, then we won't argue."

"My negative character traits are truly negative. I'll work on refining my character and then the root will be taken care of and we'll get along."

"That's absolutely correct. I need to learn how to be different. And then we'll get along just fine."

"Those outside observers are right in agreeing that I am totally wrong and you are totally right. I'll switch my entire way of thinking, speaking, and acting to the way that you do and then we'll have peace."

If you are fortunate enough to meet someone who responds this way, then making these statements will result in peace. But the reason there are so many quarrels in the world is because the standard reaction to blaming is counter-blaming.

Whenever you find yourself in a conflict, ask yourself, "What can I say or do that might be a solution to this situation?"

In the vast majority of situations, refraining from blaming prevents a situation from getting worse. And then your mind is more likely to be free to think of potential solutions.

*A fellow who was married for over ten years shared with me, "I grew up in a home where my father would always try to pin the blame on someone for anything that went wrong. 'Whose fault is it?' he would frequently say.*

*"I thought that this is the correct and normal way to respond. So after I was married, I would frequently say, 'Whose fault is it?' My wife would respond, 'It's more your fault than mine. And anyway, why do we need to keep finding fault?'*

*"It seemed so natural for me to ask this question that I thought it was obvious: After we find out whose fault it is, then the problem will just take care of itself. It's now amazing to me how long*

*it took me to realize that it's usually counterproductive to ask the fault-finding, blaming question. Once I developed the new habit of asking, 'What solution can we think of?' everything went much more smoothly."*

# 7

# "WHAT'S THE BEST OPTION FOR DEALING WITH THIS?"

Each situation can be dealt with in many ways. Some ways are positive, sensible, and beneficial. These might be simple ways or creative ways. But the common factor is that the options are conducive to peace.

Other options will cause difficulties with others and problems for yourself. These options are counterproductive and problematic and will cause or prolong quarrels.

Keep asking yourself the question, "What's the best option for dealing with this?"

Using the word "option" tells you that there are always a number of choices. And using the word "best" implies that some options are better than others. When we are calm and clear-minded this appears to be obvious. But it's not so obvious to someone who is irritated, upset, or angry.

Practice brainstorming to come up with numerous approaches to solve interpersonal difficulties. When you brainstorm, you write down every idea that comes to mind, even if at first glance it might seem totally impractical. An idea that might seem silly or just a joke might have a kernel of truth. It might lead the way to finding a valid and workable solution.

You can even brainstorm with a group of friends or family members. You might present an outline of the challenges you are having with an anonymous person, without going into details and without saying anything negative, and members of the group could brainstorm with you. Together you might find a few potential solutions to resolve those challenges and create a peaceful interaction. With the input you receive, you might find solutions to thorny and complex difficulties.

Whenever you ask yourself, "What's the best option for dealing with this?" your brain will automatically tell you that certain options are definitely not approaches you should take. Even if you don't come up with a workable solution by brainstorming, knowing what not to do is a tremendous gain.

*I spoke to someone who would frequently get into quarrels. "It's not my fault," he said. "I have to call a spade a spade. I tell people straightforwardly how it is. I do things according to standard operating procedures and I expect others to do the same. If they don't, they are going to hear my thoughts on the matter."*

*I suggested that he try to think of various options and not to just repeat the same patterns. He felt that I was asking him not to be himself. I politely suggested that his essence is not the patterns that he happens to use, and it will in no way negate his essential being to try out other options. But he refused to accept what I and others told him. His inflexibility was clearly the cause of his difficulties with other people, but he preferred to blame them rather than look for better options. Hopefully he will eventually decide to think of and apply wiser options.*

*Don't put your foot in your mouth, by speaking less*

# 8

# BE CONCISE AND FOCUS ON YOUR OUTCOME

IN MANY SITUATIONS, BY SPEAKING LESS YOU WILL accomplish more.

One of the biggest mistakes people make when they argue with others is that they go on and on, for much too long. Frequently the other person isn't really listening. He is just waiting for his turn to deliver his soliloquy.

The longer one speaks when there is a quarrel, the more likely it is that he will say things that would have been better not said. Reminding a person of his past mistakes and errors is usually not conducive to resolving issues. Pointing out to a person how he reminds you of this or that difficult-to-get-along-with person is usually not conducive to resolving issues. Putting a person down, speaking condescendingly, and adding lengthy stories and metaphors is usually not conducive to resolving issues.

The short formula to keep in mind during a quarrel is: Be concise and focus on your outcome.

Omit unnecessary words. Let each word count. Each word should be part of what you need to say to reach your outcome.

Clarify the outcome you wish to achieve before you begin to speak. Keep it in mind while you are talking. Keep asking yourself the question, "Will this help me reach the outcome I want?" Remember at all times that you are not speaking in an empty room. You have a listening audience. And the purpose of your speaking is to communicate a message to the listener. His reaction to what you say is not a minor part of the communication. Rather, it is the essence of it. If you don't care at all how he reacts, why talk to him? Go to an empty room and just speak. At times this can be an effective tool to let off steam. But when you want to speak to another person to resolve quarrels and to create harmony, only say what you think will be helpful for reaching your goal.

One reason many people are not concise is because they are waiting for a response from the other person and that person doesn't offer any feedback. In many situations, if the speaker continues talking, there is less of a chance of him being successful with his communication. When you want feedback that is not spontaneously offered, keep asking questions such as, "Does this make sense to you?" "Do you agree with this?" "What are your thoughts on what I just said?" "How do you see it?"

*"I considered myself a good speaker," someone related, "but somehow when I got into a quarrel, I frequently didn't get my points across as successfully as I wanted. I couldn't understand*

why. When I taught in school, the students liked my classes. I was very clear and gave many examples.

"I spoke to an expert in communication and he asked me to give him examples of how I would speak to others. I even had him listen to my side of the conversation on the telephone when I was in the middle of an argument. He opened my eyes by telling me that I went on and on for way too long. The stories and analogies I gave were perfect for explaining my lessons in class. But they were a waste of time when I was in the middle of an argument. He asked me how often someone said to me, 'The parable you just said is exactly what I needed to hear to agree with you. Now I realize that I am wrong, and you are right.' I had to acknowledge that this didn't usually happen. His message to me was: Know your goal and keep it short. This was so important for me to hear that I pasted it near my telephone."

· What is my goal in this discussion?
- What's my/the purpose?

# 9

# KING SOLOMON'S WISE FORMULA

I N *PROVERBS* (27:19), WE FIND AN AMAZING FORMULA FOR peace. "As in water, face to face, so too is the heart of one person to another."

When you look at your reflection in a pond or in a mirror, you will see the exact same expression that is on your face. If you frown and scowl, you will see a frown and scowl staring right back at you. And if you smile and wave, you will see a smile and a wave. This is a natural law of physics. To frown and expect to see a smile in the mirror isn't a wise expectation.

King Solomon teaches us that this natural law has a counterpoint in the laws of human nature. The inner feelings you experience towards someone will be reflected back to you from the heart of that person.

See the good in other people. See them as souls who have high aspirations, even if at present they are not yet using all of their potential. See people as they will be when they are at their best. Judge people favorably. See the positive intentions of what they say and do, even when it would be preferable if they chose better ways to accomplish those positive intentions.

The way to influence people to feel better towards you is to radiate unconditional love and respect towards them. When someone likes and respects you first, it's easier to reciprocate those feelings. It is a step towards greatness to be the one to create unconditional love and respect when you need to sustain it in the face of challenges. Be willing to take this step.

*There was a person who was angry at me because he mistakenly thought that I had acted against his interests. I had told him that he was mistaken, and he told me that I was lying. He wasn't a bit open to hear the reality: Someone had said something in my name that wasn't true. I felt bad about this and his angry state put me in an unresourceful state. I decided to inwardly feel as positively as I could and would greet him in a friendly way. I kept this up and we ended up on good terms.*

# 10

# WHO IS AN
# HONORABLE PERSON?

**A** MAJOR UNDERLYING ISSUE IN MANY QUARRELS IS THAT people feel that someone else didn't treat them with the proper respect. The specific details of the quarrel are trivial compared to the fundamental need to be treated with respect.

"Who is an honorable person?" ask the Sages (*Pirkei Avos* 4:1). "The one who shows honor and respect to others." That is, your honor and respect do not depend on how others treat you. Rather, the more honor and respect that you express to others, the more honorable you yourself are. We all want to be treated with basic respect. As we internalize the essential message of the Sages, we will decrease our concern about how others treat us and we will increase our concern about how we treat others.

Be an honorable person. Show honor and respect in words and actions to others. Make this such an integral part of who you are that this is your spontaneous way of speaking and acting. Respect starts with your thoughts. Realize that each person is created in the Almighty's image. Each person has a soul with great potential. Each person has qualities that can be respected.

The more difficult it is to treat someone with respect, the more honorable you are. Let this motivate you to experience an inner respect to even the most challenging people with whom you need to interact. Even if you haven't treated someone with the respect due to each human and are already in the midst of a quarrel, by accessing a respectful way of thinking, speaking, and acting you will be able to find a solution to quarrels that arise.

*I asked a number of people, "Did you ever feel angry towards someone and then changed your feelings?" Many people replied, "Yes." "What did you or the other person do or say to make the change?" I asked. An answer that sticks out in my mind is, "I disliked someone greatly. I was very critical of him and, I have to admit, a bit envious. But he began to treat me with great respect. At first I said to myself, 'He won't keep this up.' He did, however. I began to see him in a much better light and now I actually feel good whenever I meet him."*

# 11
# My Partner in Personal Growth

VIEW PEOPLE WITH WHOM YOU ARE LIKELY TO QUARREL as your partners in personal growth. They are likely to make you more aware of your vulnerabilities, limitations, and mistakes. Don't let this get you down. Rather, let it serve as your coach. You now have more awareness of what you need to strengthen, fix, and keep on developing.

Your partner in personal growth will be able to point out ways that you are improving. Even if he doesn't explicitly give you positive feedback, you yourself will be able to notice your progress. Keep noticing when you are able to remain calmer, even though you would prefer that he speak differently. Keep noticing when you speak in ways that are more conducive to getting along better.

There is a level of kindness that is known as *chesed shel emes,* that is, kindness of truth. This is a kindness that you do totally unconditionally, a kindness you do for someone who won't be able to help you back in any way. Acting kindly towards someone who will do you favors in return is still an act of kindness but when you gain absolutely nothing from an act of kindness, that kindness is purer and more elevated. If you speak and act with kindness towards someone with whom you lack peace, your kindness is an act of personal growth. In this manner, this person serves as your partner to help you develop spiritually.

Viewing a potential adversary as your partner in personal growth will automatically make you feel better towards this person. And the more progress you make in treating this person better, the more likely it is that you will also notice that this person is treating you better. And even if he doesn't, you are still growing.

*With most people I am able to get along very smoothly. I am usually calm and friendly and so are they. But there are a few people I find infuriating. I tended to blame them for getting me off center. "These are difficult people," I would label them.*

*It was suggested that I upgrade the way I perceived them. "Each one of these individuals serves as your personal trainer. They are training you to gain greater mastery over your emotional states. They are training you to communicate better even when you find it difficult. They are training you to refine your character traits."*

Once I integrated this view, I found them less challenging. I even look forward to interacting with some of them.

# 12

# FROM THE PERSPECTIVE OF
# OUR FATHER, OUR KING

VIEWING PEACE AND QUARRELS FROM THE PERSPECTIVE of our Father, our King, Creator and Sustainer of the universe, changes the way we see things. The question we now ask ourselves is, "What would my Father, my King, want me to say and do right now?"

Parents want their children to get along well with each other. They find it extremely distressful if their children quarrel. And there is tremendous pleasure in seeing your children interacting harmoniously. This is a metaphor for understanding peace and quarrels from the perspective of our Father, our King.

If someone you respected greatly were present when you interacted with someone you were about to engage in a quarrel, the observer would definitely influence the way you spoke. You would certainly be careful to edit what you say and watch your tone of voice. Remember a time this happened to you. Awareness of the presence of the Almighty will have an even greater influence on what you say and how you say it.

Let the desire to make a great impression serve as a strong motivator. If you wanted to make a great impression on someone who is related to a person you find challenging, and you would benefit greatly by making peace, that would serve as a strong motivator to speak with respect. Let this serve as a guide to doing all that you can to make peace with the challenging children of the Creator.

From the Almighty's perspective, your making peace between two of His children who are involved in a quarrel gives Him *nachas* (pleasure and pride). A taste of this is the *nachas* parents have when they are proud of their children for great achievements. The great people who experienced this desire to give our Father, our King, *nachas* lived on a high plane of existence. This consciousness is available to all. The more you experience this, the greater you become.

*A great rabbi was walking in the direction of two people who were engaged in a vehement dispute. He thought of walking in a different direction to avoid causing them feelings of embarrassment when they would see him. But he decided that this was a wonderful opportunity to teach them a lesson.*

*When the two people saw the rabbi, they immediately lowered their voices and spoke more respectfully to each other.*

*As the rabbi came close to them, he said with a friendly smile, "I am happy to have a part in motivating you to interact with mutual respect. The more you are consistently aware of the Almighty's presence, the easier it will be for you to maintain positive ways of interacting, even though you disagree with each other."*

# 13

# PRAY FOR PEACE

WHAT ARE YOU DOING FOR PEACE? WE CAN'T ALWAYS find magical solutions that will transform former adversaries into being great friends, but we can always pray for peace.

We can pray to find peace in our own lives. We can ask our loving Father and powerful King, Creator and Sustainer of the universe, to help us have harmonious relationships with others.

We can pray to the Almighty, asking Him to help specific people bury the hatchet and smoke a peace pipe together, metaphorically, of course.

We can pray to the Almighty for peace for our People and for all the nations of the world.

Every prayer has some effect. Every prayer elevates us spiritually. Every prayer connects us with the Creator of the universe and helps us gain a much more expansive perspective.

Wherever you are and whatever your situation, use your own words to speak to your loving Father and powerful King, and ask Him for all that you need. Peace is one of the greatest needs, so along with anything else that you need, you always need peace.

And may our Father, our King, accept all our prayers for peace and bring true peace to the entire world.

*A great Sage was once asked, "You've prayed for peace for so long. Don't you get tired of praying for something that seems so far away?"*

*He answered, "If I knew that the very next prayer would accomplish all that we've prayed for, would I stop right before my prayers were answered? Moreover, since I pray for peace, it motivates me to do all that I can to help people resolve quarrels. Only then can I feel that my prayers are sincere."*

## 14

# "HOW DID I CONTRIBUTE?"

IF YOU ARE INVOLVED IN A QUARREL WITH ANOTHER PERSON, it's easy to think that it's entirely his fault. The wrong things that this person said and did are loud and clear to you. It's not easy to be aware of what you personally said or did that was wrong.

A question to keep asking yourself about any quarrel you become involved in is, "How did I contribute to this?"

Even if you feel that the other person is one hundred percent wrong, and you are one hundred percent right, you might have said or done something that was a partial cause of the quarrel, or at least a cause of it becoming as heated and bitter as it did. You might have been totally right in what you said or did, and didn't have any way to know how the other person would react. By asking how you contributed, factors and patterns might emerge that you can eliminate in the future.

*I had an ongoing feud with a close relative of mine. I felt that he was totally at fault. He repeatedly told me that I was to blame for the whole thing. I felt that he was only saying this because he couldn't acknowledge the truth, but deep down he knew he had caused the feud.*

*We went to an insightful Talmudic scholar to hear his opinion. He listened to both sides and said, "You're both going about this mistakenly. Each one of you has contributed to the problem. You both need to ask yourself, 'What have I done already to contribute to the quarre?' Then ask yourselves, 'What can I do now to improve the situation?' "... Thinking this over later, we both realized that he was right. This was a major breakthrough in resolving our dispute.*

# 15

# THE DRAMA
# OF QUARRELS

THERE ARE INDIVIDUALS WHO ENJOY THE STIMULATION and drama of quarrels to such an extent that they purposely try to stir them up. They will do what they can to provoke arguments. In the extreme, they will purposely go to both factions and tell them that the other is speaking and acting against them.

Will some who enjoy creating skirmishes and battles read a book about avoiding and resolving quarrels? Not likely, but perhaps he might. So if any reader recognizes himself, I hope he will make a committed resolution to overcome this addicting form of stimulation. To make amends, he can now try to promote peace with all his inner strength and ingenuity. It takes a certain amount of understanding of human nature to purposely provoke quarrels; it takes even more understanding of human nature to make peace. Let the reader feel stimulated by this challenge.

If you personally are far from this vice, be careful not to allow yourself to fall prey to someone who gains enjoyment and pleasure from your quarrels. Either confront the person directly, or avoid saying anything to him that could get back to the other side.

Many people who like quarrels won't necessarily be blatantly contentious. They might make subtle comments designed to get you angry at another person. Don't take the bait. A fish might grab a tasty looking worm, but the hook to catch him is just waiting. As an intelligent human being, you can have more awareness.

Those who enjoy the stimulation of a quarrel might be able to find a kosher way to meet this need. They can enjoy intellectual debates. They should choose to debate others who can fend for themselves and who also enjoy lively and heated discussions.

*I listened to a professional reporter interview a number of politicians on controversial issues. His comments and questions were clearly designed to make his show more interesting to the listeners. I noted the patterns. He would say things like, "Don't you think it was wrong of so and so to say or do such and such?" and, "He said this about you. What do you say about him?" I also noted the patterns of people who were meticulously careful to discuss only the issues. No matter how hard the interviewer tried, they were steadfast in their refusal to say anything personal against others. This has served as a role model for how to handle similar situations.*

# 16
# AARON'S STRATEGY

THERE IS A WELL-KNOWN MIDRASH THAT DESCRIBES Aaron's strategy for making peace between people. Aaron, who was the first High Priest and Moses' older brother, was an expert at helping people who were quarreling overcome their negative feelings.

What would Aaron do? When he heard that two people were quarreling, he would approach one and tell him, "I heard Reuven say positive things about you." And then he would go to Reuven and tell him, "I heard Shimon say positive things about you." The next time Reuven and Shimon met they would smile at each other, and this would create positive feelings between them.

Can't this approach backfire? Imagine telling someone that another person really likes him, and then repeating a similar message to the other. Isn't it possible that when they would see each other, each one will say, "I don't know why that person said this to you. It's not true."

It seems likely that Aaron would actually elicit some positive statements from both people. Then when he told each of them that the other said something positive about them, it was totally true.

When you want to emulate Aaron, you can ask:

"What are some of the positive qualities this other person has?"

"What are the positive things that this person has done for you that you have appreciated?"

"What are some of the acts of kindness that this person has done for others?"

"What have you liked about this person?"

"If this person would sincerely apologize to you, would you then want to resolve the quarrel?"

The answers to these and similar questions will give you positive material to convey to both parties. When people hear that someone is speaking positively about them, they tend to like that person.

*Someone told me that because of a quarrel he and another person didn't get along very well, but he wanted to improve the relationship. He went over to someone he felt was extremely reliable, and told him, "I am going to tell you a number of positive things about this person. I will tell you how much I respect him and the qualities he has that I appreciate. Please do me a favor and repeat these things to him." This proved to be highly effective, and the two people renewed their friendship.*

# 17

# THE MOST COMMON MISTAKE OF OUTSIDERS

ONE PARTY COMES OVER TO YOU AND TELLS YOU THE negative things someone else said or did. You experience righteous anger. This person is certainly right, the other person is certainly wrong. You might tell your source, "I agree with you. He's an awful person." You might censure the other person, "You are an awful person." You might tell others, "That person is an awful person."

Did you hear both sides in the presence of both parties before forming any opinion? If not, the Torah considers what you heard as a "false report." (The Chofetz Chaim elaborates on this in his class work. See *Prohibitions*, no. 2.)

"The map is not the territory." This basic principle of General Semantics applies to every story and report you ever hear. Details are always left out. Words describing any situation are never an exact portrait of any interaction. What was the entire context? What were the exact words that were used by both sides? What was the exact tone of voice of each segment of the exchange? Even when someone reports what he himself said with total accuracy, the tone of voice totally transforms the energy that was exchanged. What were the facial expressions? What were the intentions, motivations, and assumptions?

King Solomon compares an outsider getting involved in an argument that is not his to a passerby who pulls the ear of a dog (*Proverbs* 26:17). The calm dog was harmless. Pull his ear and you'll have problems. Taking sides in a quarrel that's not yours is even worse when you don't really have the entire picture. Those who impulsively take sides often don't realize how many mistakes they will be making.

Every word an outsider says to a party in a quarrel can make the situation either better or worse. Whenever someone tells you about a situation that is either already a quarrel or could easily lead to a quarrel, ask yourself, "What can I say now that will be conducive to peace?" And when the answer is, "I don't really know," keep quiet. It's a major mistake to make things worse.

*I spoke to someone who claimed that one party to a quarrel was totally right. He was passionate in defending one side and condemning the other side. "How many times and for how long did you speak to both sides in the presence of the other?"*

*"Well," he said, "with all due modesty, I'm good at telling who is right even when I don't speak to both sides."*

*"How would you feel if someone else totally accepted another person's version of a quarrel that he had with you, without hearing your side of the argument? And even if he eventually*

*did hear it, he had already made up his mind against you before he ever spoke to you. Would you think that he was making a mistake?"*

"That's different," he said.

"The only difference is that if you personally were involved, it's quite clear to you that it's a mistake to form an opinion without hearing both sides."

# 18

# YOUR SELF-IMAGE CREATES YOU

Y OUR SELF-IMAGE CREATES YOU. IDENTIFY YOUR IDEALS, values, and highest aspirations. This affects the way you think, the way you speak, and the actions you will and won't do.

View yourself as a person who loves and pursues peace. View yourself as someone with intrinsic worth and dignity. View yourself as someone who is a child of the Creator and has been created in His image. You are too distinguished to be petty.

People who haven't yet upgraded their self-image might feel that their self-esteem is threatened if someone doesn't speak to them the way they would wish. If self-esteem is low, even minor slights and oversights might be perceived as personal attacks on one's very being. With low self-esteem, someone might take offense when no offense was intended.

Since self-image refers to the way you personally view your-self, your present view of yourself is the only factor that makes the difference. When someone is young, the subjective opin-ions of others has a major influence on self-image. But once you are old enough to think for yourself, you can transcend any limiting ideas of who you are. As you keep upgrading your self-image, you will find your goals, your traits, and your emotional states also being upgraded.

As you view yourself as a person who loves and pursues peace, this will help you avoid quarrels and will motivate you to help others who are quarreling to make peace.

The very fact that you are reading this book means that you are a person who considers peace important. Even if you only avoided one or two quarrels, it makes you eligible to view yourself as someone who goes out of his way for peace. As soon as you try to help people make peace even once, you are entitled to identify yourself as someone who wants peace. You are adding a peace consciousness to your identity.

*Someone once asked me to join him in approaching two people who were involved in a bitter dispute.*

*"But I'm not assertive," I protested. "I'm not the type of person who can just contact people and talk to them about peace."*

*"But if I can do it, so can you," my friend said encouragingly.*

*"But making peace is who you are and not who I am," I defended my lack of initiative.*

*"When we were both one day old, neither of us had a clear definition who we were. Our actions create our self-image, just as our self-image creates our actions," he told me. "I spoke to a number of people, attempting to make peace. Sometimes I've been successful and sometimes not. The same way that my actions have helped me*

*view myself as someone who pursues peace, you too can begin to view yourself as someone who pursues peace as soon as you join me even once. Even before we actually speak to anyone, the willingness to approach someone automatically makes you a person who wants to create peace."*

*He was right. After I went with him that one time, I looked at myself as someone who is willing to do the difficult for the sake of peace.*

# 19

# SELF-IMAGE MIGHT CAUSE UNAWARENESS

SOME PEOPLE MIGHT VIEW THEMSELVES AS PEACE-LOVING, as easy to get along with, as always being well-intentioned, as being spiritual or elevated. They might therefore refuse to acknowledge their part in causing a quarrel.

"I'm not someone who gets angry and quarrels," they might claim. "Therefore any quarrels I do get into are always the other person's fault."

It's important to try to be as objective as possible. Even if you only find yourself in one quarrel, you might have said or done something that caused it or prolonged it. All the more so if you find yourself in a number of quarrels.

You might not have intended to say anything that is quarrelsome, but perhaps you said something you shouldn't have said. Someone else might have taken offense about something you said or did even though you didn't realize it. Be open to the feedback of others. The more awareness you gain, the more careful you will be able to be.

People who truly and sincerely want peace will be open to the possibility that they might have caused a lack of peace inadvertently. While they would have preferred to avoid it, they will acknowledge it. This will enable them to prevent similar occurrences in the future.

*I attended a lecture on increasing our sensitivity to how we might be causing others pain. The lecturer said he had been told that he had caused some extreme emotional pain without realizing it. He gave oral tests to a thirteen-year-old who wanted to be accepted to his high school. A parent called him up and angrily said, "Why did you embarrass and humiliate my son?"*

*The lecturer was flabbergasted. He was always careful to give each student a positive feeling, even if he didn't feel that a particular student would be accepted to his school.*

*He called the boy up to apologize and to find out what he had said to hurt the boy. He was certain that the boy's reaction was totally unfounded.*

*Apparently, when he was testing the boy's knowledge, he had written the boy's name on a blank paper and then unmindfully doodled on that page. The boy noticed the marks that he made, and assumed that the teacher wasn't a bit interested in what he had to say. The boy felt that he had been misjudged immediately and wasn't given a fair chance.*

*The scholarly and kind teacher explained to the boy that he didn't even realize he was doodling. It definitely didn't imply anything about the boy and his capabilities. The teacher reassured the boy that he had learned a lesson and wouldn't doodle during tests ever again.*

## 20
# TONE OF VOICE

TONE OF VOICE IS THE KEY ELEMENT THAT DISTINGUISHES an angry quarrel from a peaceful discussion. Master your tone of voice and you have mastered the number one key for preventing quarrels. Even if someone else raises his voice, when your voice remains calm, his tone of voice will eventually become calmer. (Of course, the content of what you say will play a major role in how the other person will react, and is discussed in other sections of this book.)

Everyone realizes that when one sings, one's tone of voice will make a major difference. Two people can sing the same melody, but the quality can be worlds apart. A world-class tone of voice brings out a very different reaction in the listeners than a screeching one.

"The words of the wise are heard gently" (*Koheles* 9:17). We speak to others because we have some goal. We want others to agree with us. We want to motivate and influence others to either do or refrain from doing something. We want others to understand us even if they don't agree. A wise person focuses on outcomes (Tractate *Tomid* 32). Choose the tone of voice that is best for the situation. In the vast majority of situations, we are heard best when we speak gently.

Record your voice. First, sound as angry as you can. Shout and scream. After doing this for a few minutes, sound as kind and compassionate as you can. Speak the way you speak when you respect someone. Speak the way you speak when you are totally rational and logical, with warmth added into the equation.

Then listen to the tape. Ask yourself the question: "What tone of voice would I prefer that others use when they speak to me?" Hillel's well-known statement applies here, "Don't do unto others what you would not want them to do to you." Speak as respectfully to others as you would want them to speak to you. This has tremendous power to prevent quarrels and arguments, as the Ramban wrote in his famous ethical letter.

But what if it's difficult to speak pleasantly? Do the same thing that professional cantors, singers, and bar-mitzvah boys do: They practice. And when they want to give an especially great performance, they practice a lot. The benefits of peace are so great and peace is such a big mitzvah that all the time you invest in practicing is time wisely spent.

If someone raises his voice to you, you can respectfully say, "I hear better with a lower volume."

*Someone once came to Rabbi Eliezer Shach, the late Rosh Hayeshiva of Ponevez, to speak about some difficulties he was having in getting along with his wife. Rabbi Shach advised him, "You are speaking to me very respectfully and pleasantly right now. Be totally resolved to consistently speak to your wife the same way."*

*Think of someone you greatly respect and how you would speak to that person. Then remember to apply this pattern if you are ever tempted to speak disrespectfully to someone.*

# 21
# TONE DOWN RHETORIC

THE LANGUAGE YOU USE WHEN YOU HAVE A CONFLICT OF interests with someone can either increase the tensions between you and the other party, or it can decrease it. It all depends on your choice of words.

There are words about which someone could easily say, "Those are fighting words." Avoid them. What exactly would constitute "fighting words" will of course depend on the reaction of the listener. Don't needlessly offend the other person. It's intrinsically wrong, and you will end up losing out.

Avoid threats. If you threaten the other side, they might become intimidated and step down from their position, or they might threaten you in return. Then both sides might be heading into a battle that neither side really wants. And even if the other party is intimidated, does this approach really build your character or lower it? There might be situations when intimidation is necessary, but save this for the rare occasion when there is no other alternative. As my friend Bob Burg points out in his book, *Winning Without Intimidation,* there are many patterns of speaking with respect to other people that can influence them to be reasonable without using any form of intimidation whatsoever.

Toning down your rhetoric doesn't ensure you that things will work out the way you want. But it will prevent quarrels from becoming nasty and mean.

*I grew up in a very rough neighborhood. It was a place where many disagreements got out of hand and turned into fights. Sometimes both the "winner" and the loser ended up in the hospital. But I personally was never involved in a fight. What was the secret? No matter what anyone said, I never said anything to escalate the intensity of the dialogue.*

# 22

# COMMUNICATION
## AS A LOOP

XPERT COMMUNICATORS VIEW COMMUNICATION AS A loop. This is especially important when you find yourself in a quarrel. Incompetent communicators view communication as, "I told him exactly what I thought and if he doesn't like what I said or the way I said it, it's his problem."

A loop means that every statement you make sets up the statement that the other person will make. You can easily blame the other person for not speaking to you the way that you would like. You can easily blame the other person for not being reasonable. You can easily blame the other person for getting angry. You can easily blame the other person for not listening to what you have to say. All this can be true. However, when you view your communication as a loop, you stop blaming the other person and you begin to think more efficiently and effectively.

The number one thought in a peaceful communication loop is, "What can I say and how can I say it to bring out a peaceful response from this person?"

When you view communication as a loop, what kind of response do you think you might get if *you* were to say to someone:

"You're an idiot for saying that."

"That's a stupid remark."

"We wouldn't be arguing now if you weren't here."

"If you would have better character traits, it would be much easier to get along with you."

"I don't know why I even try speaking to you. It's a total waste of my time."

If you tell the person that you think he is an idiot, will that make him more intelligent and reasonable? If you tell someone that his remark was stupid, is his next remark likely to be on the brilliant side? If you tell someone that you wouldn't be arguing if he weren't there, isn't he likely to think, "Well, if *you* weren't here now, we wouldn't be arguing?" Will telling someone that he needs better character traits immediately help him create or access better character traits? If you tell someone that it's a waste of your time to talk to him, will that help put him in a calm and friendly state, making him more agreeable and pleasant to interact with?

The answers to these questions are quite obvious when we see them in print. But when we are in a quarrel with someone, we are likely to say things that help maintain a negative loop. Be prepared in advance. Keep asking yourself, "What can I say and how can I say it to create a positive loop?"

Even if you can't think of what to say to create a positive loop in a given situation, just realizing that you are creating a loop is more likely to prevent you from saying things that will make the loop more negative.

*I couldn't speak to someone without getting frustrated and angry. This person had a knack for saying things that would get me off balance. I witnessed this person interact with others and I saw how this person was an expert at creating negative loops. I realized that I was critical of this person and I wanted to think of this person in more positive terms. I then decided that I would view this person as my teacher and coach. Every time I saw this person I would use the interaction as a lesson to remember to create positive loops when I spoke to others. And when I spoke to this person, I was so dedicated to creating a positive loop that I found things to say that actually brought out pleasant responses.*

# 23
# INNER CALM FOR HARMONY WITH OTHERS

IMAGINE WHAT IT WOULD BE LIKE TO BE CONSISTENTLY calm. Imagine what it would be like to be calm right now. Either one of two things: You are either calm right now, and you know what it feels like to be calm, or you are not yet calm, and as you read this you can choose to become calm. And when you are calm, you will find it easier to interact harmoniously with others.

Allow yourself to breathe calmly. And as you do, repeat the word "calm" to yourself. Just talking about being calm enables you to become calmer. You might even choose to visualize a calm place. When you are calm, how do you know that you are calm? What is it like when you feel calm? What do you say to yourself? Imagine that the Creator gave you the gift of being calm. You might want to think of a calm role model who is also empowered and accomplishes a lot. Regardless of how you do it, choose to be calm right now.

When you are calm yourself, you talk in a calmer way to others. This is conducive to peace. Your remaining calm when interacting with someone else will have a calming effect on that person. When you experience inner calm, you think more clearly about the wisest thing to say and do.

When people quarrel, they access states that are the opposite of being calm. Even if you are calm in the beginning, it's a challenge to remain calm when the other person is saying things that tend to push your buttons. And that is why it's so important to keep practicing the skill of accessing calm states. The greater your mastery at this skill, the more inner harmony you will experience yourself and the easier it will be for you to have peaceful discussions with others. With enough practice, you will even be able to remain calm in situations that usually cause you to lose your cool.

*I've always looked at myself as a peaceful person. But I noticed that there are times when the way I speak brings out the worst in the people who mean the most to me. This is when I feel stressed out and overwhelmed. I used to say, "It's not my fault I'm talking like this. I have a valid reason for being stressed."*

*I spoke to a counselor about this and I was told, "Forget about whether or not it's your fault. Rather, focus on your ability as a human being to master the states you want to master. This takes focus. And you will succeed when you decide that this is a high priority for you. Calmly repeat the word, 'calm,' for about two minutes at a time, five times a day. I realize that ten minutes can seem like a long time. But when you waste time arguing and quarreling, you waste much more time. Not only during the quarreling, but also during the amount of time you waste obsess-*

*ing about what you and the other person both said when you weren't calm."*

*This made sense to me, but I didn't have the patience to practice this exercise. Then one day when I was stressed, I was so upset with the way I spoke and acted when I was angry, that I said, "That's it. I am totally committed to doing this exercise daily for at least thirty days." I followed through and this has made a major difference in my life. I no longer blame my anger on my stress. Rather, stress is a signal for me to repeat the word, "calm," until I feel my entire nervous system becoming calmer and more peaceful. When I'm in a calm state, I think much more clearly about what would be the best things to say and do.*

# 24
# WIN-WIN APPROACH

ONFLICTS OF INTEREST ARE INEVITABLE. BITTER
quarrels are not. Master the ability to negotiate with a
friendly style. Your positive approach to negotiations
will have a positive influence on the patterns of the other person.

When searching for solutions to conflicts of interest, think
win-win. That is, how to resolve the conflict in a way that both
parties gain, even if neither gets his way entirely.

A simple example would be if two partners argue over what
approach to take to expand their business. One partner loves to
take risks and is willing to risk a lot in the hope of gaining a lot.
The other partner values security. He would rather gain a much
smaller profit as long as the moves he makes are relatively safe
and secure. In an argument, each one's initial position is dia-
metrically opposite the other's. To work together, they need to
do something where there is risk, but where the potential loss
would not be as great as the risk-taker had wanted, yet where
there was less certainty than the security-oriented partner orig-
inally desired. Since both parties' positions are taken into consideration, this would be a win-win solution.

If a parent wants to take a few children on an enjoyable out-
ing and they differ about where to go, they can decide that

they will go to a place that they will all enjoy, even though this wasn't the original request of any of them. Or they might decide that this time they will go to one place, and next time they will go to the other place.

Keep asking yourself, "What would be a win-win solution in the present situation?" And suggest to the person with whom you differ, "I want you to be happy with the solution we come up with, and I want my needs to be met also. So let's brainstorm together for win-win solutions." It will be difficult for most people to say to you, "I don't want it your way at all. I want it win-lose." It's much more likely that the other person will respond, "Since you want to make it beneficial for me, I agree to make it beneficial for you, too."

*I used to feel that if I gave in to someone's demands then I was a loser, and I didn't want to be a loser. So even if something was a relatively small matter, I would argue and argue. I realized that I was wasting a lot of time on inconsequential matters, but I felt I couldn't always let others have their way. What helped me greatly was a conflict of interest I got into with someone who has a reputation of getting along well with almost everyone. I was ready to argue as long as it took for this person to agree with me, but he said with a sincere smile, "I would like for us to find a solution that will satisfy you and let me go away with a good feeling, too." I didn't feel that I would be a loser at all when we found a solution that made us both feel good. And I've tried this pattern many times since then with frequent positive results.*

# 25
# AGREEMENT FRAME

THERE IS A PATTERN KNOWN AS AN AGREEMENT FRAME THAT is a wise pattern to master. The opposing frames are argument frames, quarrel frames, disagreement frames, critical frames, and obnoxious frames. These are patterns that easily cause unpleasant disagreements.

Let's take a look at patterns that are the opposite of agreement frames:

Someone says: "Today is a nice today."

Disagreement frame: "What's so nice about it? Many days have been nicer. This won't last. And I can think of at least ten ways the day could have been better."

Someone says: "I feel that I have been improving."

Disagreement frame: "You still have a long way to go. You should have improved a long time ago. And so what if you're improving? Don't be so arrogant and conceited and boast so much about it."

Someone says: "I gained a lot from that talk."

Disagreement frame: "There was so much to criticize about that talk, why do you only focus on how you've gained? How do you know for certain that you've gained? Maybe you only think that you have gained. And even if you've gained, the gain probably won't last very long."

Two scholars with mutual respect who are involved in a discussion might find it appropriate to just comment on points of disagreement. And some people relish a good argument. They have intellectual fun when they engage in verbal skirmishes. But as a general rule, being on the receiving end of nothing but critical frames is highly distressful. Yes, there is a place for criticism, disagreements, and diverse opinions, but there isn't a place for being obnoxious.

Agreement frames are when you begin by commenting on something with which you agree. You mention points of agreement right at the beginning.

For example, with the above-mentioned statements, agreement frames would be:

"Yes. Today is a great day. There are many things to appreciate about it."

"I can see that you having been devoting time and effort to improving, and you are making noticeable progress. I wish you success in keeping it up."

"There are many points with which I agree, and there is a lot to gain from internalizing those points."

If you first express something with which you agree, and then when you word your disagreements with respect, you are more likely to have a peaceful discussion.

*I spoke to someone who is an expert at serving as a mediator. He has been highly successful at teaching people how to discuss disagreements peacefully. "What do you consider the most important tool that you use?" I asked him.*

*"I constantly look for points of agreement. I find what both parties have in common and factors that they both agree on. When I deal with family members, I point out to them that they both want a harmonious and mutually respectful relationship. When I can influence both parties to first comment on what they agree with and to keep their common points of interest in mind, I can often change the tone and atmosphere of quarreling to the much more pleasant one of searching for acceptable solutions."*

# 26

# LEARN FROM YOUR STRENGTHS AND SUCCESSES

W E ALL CAN COMMUNICATE WELL WITH SOME people but not as well with some other people. Learn from your strengths. Learn from your successes. Learn from your best moments.

Your own best moments are your best teacher. So the question to ask yourself is, "With whom do I communicate well?" What can you learn from the way you speak to those people? Very likely, the way that those people speak to you and treat you has an influence on the way that you communicate with them. Even so, awareness of what you do correctly when you speak to them can help you speak to the people with whom you find it difficult to interact.

Moreover, if you ever have a difficult time communicating with someone with whom you sometimes communicate well, ask yourself, "What exactly did I say and do when I communicated well with this person in the past?"

One of the major keys to interacting well with someone is for you to be in a positive state yourself. Think of times and moments when you have been in states that helped you communicate well. Keep accessing those states. Remember how you spoke. Remember how you felt. Remember the look on your face, or imagine the expression on your face, when you were in a positive, resourceful, communicating state.

In the future, whenever you communicate especially well with someone, consciously add that to your brain's library of states. You might want to give that state a special name. Choose a label for that state that will remind you of the resourceful way that you spoke.

Every pattern that you use that is helpful in one context can be used again and again in other contexts. Your initial reaction in new contexts might be that you don't know what to say or do, but when you search your brain's archives for contexts when you did speak or act to your liking, you can apply them in the present context.

*Someone approached me at a wedding and said, "I have a problem interacting with a specific member of my family. Can you tell me what I need to do to improve my interactions with that person?"*

*I asked the person, "How would you like to interact with that person?"*

*"I asked you a question and instead of telling me how I can improve, you are asking me questions. Please tell me what to do," he said.*

*I repeated the question, "How would you like to interact with this person?" This time the person answered me.*

"*Think back to a time when you interacted well with this person or with someone who is similar. What did you do then?*" I asked him.

"*Again, I asked you what I should do and instead of answering me, you are asking me what I have done,*" he said in frustration.

I explained to him that I was answering him. "*I am not only showing you how to resolve the question you asked, but I'm also giving you a pattern that will help in many future situations. You first need to clarify your outcomes or goals, and then remember a time when you spoke or acted in ways that were effective.*"

A few weeks later, I met him again and asked him how things were going. With a big smile on his face, he said, "*I didn't realize right away the power and effectiveness of what you told me. I'm extremely grateful.*"

# 27

# UNDERSTANDING EVEN IF YOU DON'T AGREE

I F YOU FIND YOURSELF IN A DISAGREEMENT OR QUARREL with another person, your first step should be to try to understand him from his point of view.

What usually happens is that both parties start by trying to convince the other side to change position. "I am right and you are wrong," is the way to summarize the first step that is commonly used.

When you try to understand why someone thinks the way he does, you might find that you agree with some of the things that he is saying. You might find that you weren't aware of all the facts. You might find that the other person has made assumptions that you can easily show are not valid. And when you show understanding of the other person's position, he will usually be more open to understanding your position.

Some people are concerned, "If I try to understand the other person's position, he might assume that I agree with him." Of course, he might. But then you can explain that even though you understand him you still disagree.

When you understand why a person thinks, speaks, or acts the way he does, you will find it easier to work out peaceful solutions. The very act of being understood will usually influence the emotional state of the other person. He is likely to become calmer. Being calm, he will tend to become more reasonable.

To gain greater understanding, say, "Why do you think the way you do?" When the person does start explaining, listen to what he has to say. There is often a strong tendency to keep interrupting him and arguing. Remember that your goal is to understand him. Wait until he is finished explaining before you present your own case.

*Someone who was frequently successful at helping people get along better said that he asks both sides, "Why do you think the other person thinks the way he does?" or he will say, "Let's try to understand the other person from his point of view." Not everyone is willing to try to understand. Some will say, "They are totally wrong. They don't really have a point of view." When he tells them, "But everyone has a point of view," some say, "Well, the most evil people in history had a point of view. It's wrong to try to understand them." He tries to get them to see that even if this person spoke or acted wrongly, it's a mistake to compare him with the most evil people who ever lived. He finds that when he can get each person to understand the other side better, both sides are much more willing to reach a peaceful solution.*

# 28
# MENTAL REHEARSALS

EFORE DELIVERING AN IMPORTANT SPEECH, PEOPLE rehearse. Before performing before a large audience, people rehearse. When you rehearse, you build up your skills and you improve what needs improvement. When you practice properly, those experiences are stored in your brain cells and you can access them again and again.

Before a potentially difficult encounter with someone, mentally rehearse. In your mind's eye, imagine yourself getting along well. See yourself remaining calm and friendly the entire time. See yourself speaking with respect and kindness to the other person. Imagine that this person will speak to you in a friendly way.

This mental exercise is a powerful tool. It works either positively or negatively. If you imagine that someone will speak and act negatively towards you, this imaging will put you in an unresourceful state, and will make it more likely that you will help create that negative reality. With equal effort you can choose to utilize it positively.

But what if you don't yet see these mental rehearsals vividly? Don't be overly concerned how vividly you imagine, just imagine a positive interaction the way you would imagine anything else. Imagine in your own way that you will enjoy the interaction. Imagine that you will be in a calm state the entire time. Imagine that the other person will be at his best.

Use your brain's power to mentally rehearse before speaking in public, before teaching, before selling, before negotiating. As you master this, you will find yourself interacting more peacefully and skillfully even in highly challenging situations.

*At meetings attended by heads of the organization with which I am affiliated, I would frequently get into quarrels with one of my colleagues. I felt that his way of speaking was arrogant and demeaning. He would usually say things that got me angry. The tension between us was noticeable to everyone, and I wished I could speak more peacefully to him. But before each meeting I just "knew" that I would have a rough time with him. I asked someone for advice, and it was suggested that I mentally rehearse the meeting. I should imagine myself getting along smoothly with him the entire meeting. I should imagine myself feeling calm and relaxed and speaking with an upbeat tone of voice. I should see him having a pleasant look on his face when he spoke to me. This seemed unrealistic to me, but the person who made the suggestion insisted that I spend a few minutes before the meeting imagining this. I did and was surprised to see how smoothly our exchanges actually went.*

# 29
# TWELVE POWERFUL WORDS

THERE ARE TWELVE WORDS THAT ARE POWERFULLY effective in resolving quarrels. These twelve words are all common words that you've heard frequently, yet saying them can take inner strength and courage.

The twelve words are, "I was wrong. I made a mistake. I apologize. Please forgive me."

But what if the other person was also wrong? What if the other person also made mistakes? Shouldn't that person apologize to me? Shouldn't that person ask my forgiveness?

The answer could be, yes, the other person also made mistakes and said and did things that were wrong. Yes, the other person really should apologize and ask for forgiveness. Nevertheless, you still should apologize and ask for forgiveness for what you did wrong. We can't control someone else's behavior. It's difficult enough for us to control our own behavior.

For someone who loves and pursues peace it's a bit easier to say these twelve words than if he didn't love peace. But it will still be difficult at first. How do we get ourselves to do what is difficult? We practice.

If you repeat these words over and over again, they become easier to say. "I was wrong. I made a mistake. I apologize. Please forgive me." If you've read the last sentence, you've said these words in your mind. Terrific. You are on the way to saying this to someone else.

*I had a long conversation with someone who counseled married couples to apologize and ask for forgiveness. This is what he shared with me: "Only a minority of people who quarrel are willing to acknowledge right away that they were wrong and made mistakes. Each party wants the other one to acknowledge their mistakes first. I will often suggest that they say, 'I am sorry I caused you pain. I apologize.' Many try to start off by saying, 'If I caused you pain, I am sorry.' The other party usually doesn't appreciate this approach. 'What do you mean, "if you caused me pain," it's so obvious that you did. This is just a way to escape responsibility.' Some people do say that they are sorry and ask for forgiveness, but their tone of voice isn't very convincing. They sound as if they are just saying the words because someone is coercing them to, but their hearts aren't into them. Here people differ. Some people are so happy that the other person has made a positive effort in the right direction that they immediately say, 'And I am sorry that I caused you pain. Please forgive me.' Others argue that the tone of voice implies that they are not sorry. So I suggest to the one making the apology to mentally rehearse this over and over again and then, when they feel it, to say it. Those who do are on the road to peace."*

# 30

# REPEATING YOUR APOLOGY

SINCERE APOLOGIES ARE FREQUENTLY SUCCESSFUL IN creating peace. But what if you've apologized to someone and the person refuses to accept your apology? Doesn't this show that the other person is stubborn and will never accept an apology from you? No, it doesn't prove that at all. All it tells you is that a single apology is insufficient in this instance.

Be willing to repeat an apology over and over again. How often? As many times as it takes. You might have to wait a day or a number of days before you try again. But don't let a refusal to accept your apology prevent you from apologizing again.

Some people feel that it's demeaning. "It was hard for me to apologize in the first place. Why do I have to keep begging for my apology to be accepted?"

Seeking peace is an elevated action. It doesn't lower you to ask for forgiveness. It raises you. The more times you need to repeat your apology and you actually do so, the higher you become. If you've truly wronged the other person in a way that caused a lot of pain, you owe the other person an apology. Put in all the energy and effort that is necessary until the apology is accepted.

Be persistent. Don't give up. Don't get discouraged. If you do get discouraged, however, strengthen yourself and try again. View each time you make your request for forgiveness as a way to build your spiritual and character "muscles." People don't build physical muscles with just a few tries. It takes time. And it takes a lifetime to accomplish spiritually.

*I would gladly apologize to another person if I ever said or did anything that caused distress. But if the other person didn't immediately accept my apology, I became discouraged. What helped me was a talk I had with a person who trained people to become successful salesmen. "What do you consider the most common mistakes that people make in sales?" I asked him.*

*"They tend to give up too soon. A high percentage of sales on expensive items only happens after four or five tries. The average salesperson gives up after only one try. The truly successful salesperson is willing to try even nine and ten times when he knows that this person could really benefit greatly from what he is offering. He is willing to try again and again, as long as it takes."*

*After hearing this I realized that this is appropriate regarding apologizing.*

# 31

# "THEY" SHOULD START

A BARRIER TO MAKING PEACE WITH OTHER PEOPLE IS the feeling, "The other person should start making peace. As soon as he starts, I'll go along with it."

If you want another person to take the initiative to make peace, and he actually takes that initiative, great. Now you'll have peace. But the problem with this approach is that sometimes the other person will not take the initiative. It could be that he sees you as the one who is "really" at fault. And since you see him as the one who is "really" at fault, you will both be waiting a long time for the other one to take the initiative.

In important areas of your life, don't wait until someone else comes over to you. Be proactive. You make the necessary telephone call. You make the necessary visit. You approach the other person when you see him.

What if someone had a business, and wouldn't do anything at all to find customers? "Let them come to me; I'm not going to approach anyone else. If they want to buy real estate, they will have to make the first move. If they want insurance, let them approach me. If they want to donate money to the institution for which I am collecting, let them call me up to tell me that they want to give a large donation. Why should I have to call them up?"

It's obvious that when something is really important to you, you are willing to make an effort. A person who is ill will contact a doctor; he won't wait until a doctor happens to contact him to offer assistance. Consider it equally as important to make peace.

*In the course of a day I met two people who had lacked peace in their lives. One had resolved his problem by taking the initiative and approaching his adversary. The other one was not willing to take such initiative and was involved in a long-lasting feud. I asked them about the attitude towards peace in the homes in which they grew up.*

*The one who wasn't willing to take the initiative said, "In my home, if someone felt that the other person started the fight, he waited until the other approached him. It's not our obligation to go to that person since he started it."*

*The one who resolved the quarrel fairly quickly said, "In my home if someone was angry at you, you went over to him. It didn't matter whose fault it was."*

*Playing devil's advocate, I asked him, "But didn't people feel resentful that they had to make the first effort?"*

*"No. My father viewed making peace as a great privilege. He was happy for the opportunity to do all he could to make peace. It was a source of positive feelings."*

## 32

# WE CAN ONLY BE
# IN THE PRESENT

O NE OF THE MOST IMPORTANT PRINCIPLES FOR SELF-mastery in all areas, especially emotional mastery, is that you are always in the present. Of course, you have a past history. Learn from it. Learn from the wise things you've already done and learn from your mistakes. Of course you need to think about and plan for the future. But regardless of whether you are thinking of the past or the future, you are always doing so in the present. And in the present keep asking yourself, "What is the wisest thing to say and do right now?"

In a quarrel, both parties often say things that would have been better not said. Now, in the present, we have the power to choose to say what's best to say now. When both parties to a quarrel agree, "Let's both live in the present. Let's begin again, to speak with mutual respect in a reasonable way," then they can get over the past, and deal with the present.

"But it's not so easy to let go of the past," many people comment. And they are right. It's not easy. If it were, then everyone would do it. It makes so much sense to deal with the present and future, rather than to rehash the past. But not all brains are willing to allow their owners to do so. If you find this difficult, make it a high priority to train your brain to keep its focus on what you can say and do now that would be wise to say and do. As you keep repeating to your brain, "What can I say and do now?" this will become a habit that you will benefit from immensely.

What if you are willing to live in the present, but the other party to a quarrel feels so much distress about the past, that he or she is not yet ready to discuss the present and future? Then you need the courage and patience to discuss the past until the other person is ready to go forward. Especially when you hurt the other person more than the other person hurt you, it's relatively easy for you to say, "Let's focus on the present." But if you were more hurt than the other person, it's likely that the other person could readily tell you, "Let's focus on the present," and you might not be immediately ready to accept his sage advice.

Discuss the past to the degree it's needed to allow both parties to keep the main focus on the present. Speaking about the past can give both parties better understanding of each other, and can help them let out the emotional build-up. But the entire time keep your goal: making peace in the present.

*I met someone who used to say, "Resolving quarrels is quite easy. All you need to do is live in the present. People should forget about the mistakes and wrongs of others, and just focus on what is going on now." And then it finally happened: This person became involved in a major dispute with a couple of tough fellows. They were verbally abusive and while they didn't threaten physical violence, the looks on their faces and the way they spoke gave one a feeling that if they weren't satisfied, a few punches weren't impossible. They caused him a lot of emotional pain and distress. Then when he basically gave in to them, they blithely said to him, "Let bygones be bygones. Let's let the past go and keep doing business."*

*He was furious at the audacity of those characters. I gently said to him, "While no one can condone their behavior, they have taught you how difficult it can be to let go of the past. This will help you be more sensitive to how others also find it hard to let go of the past, even though they really know it's the wisest thing to do."*

# 33

# WHEN IT'S OVER, LET IT REMAIN OVER

N THE CLASSIC ETHICAL WORK, *ORCHOS TZADIKIM* (CH. 21), we find stated, "If two people quarreled and afterward made peace, neither should later say to the other, 'The reason I behaved as I did is because you did this and that to me.' Even if the person saying this does not intend to resume the quarrel, such a remark is apt to rekindle the dispute, since the other person will probably retort, 'No, it was really your fault.'"

It's often true that after a dispute both people blame the other not only for what the other person said, but even for what they themselves have said.

"I'm not usually the type of person who speaks or acts this way. And since I did speak and act this negatively when interacting with you, it's your fault that I did so. I wouldn't have spoken this way or acted this way if it hadn't been for you."

The need to justify ourselves is strong. Even if no one else is present, we want the other person to know that he is at fault and we aren't. But we need to overcome this pattern in order to prevent the continuation of a quarrel that has already subsided.

The more difficult it is for you not to say to the other person, "My words and actions were because of you," the greater spiritual strength you are manifesting by not saying it.

*There was a certain person with whom I would argue and argue and even when I thought the argument was over, it would still go on and on. I tried to understand why I would argue with this person for much longer periods of time than I would with others. I paid more attention to the next argument I got into with him. I realized that after we seemed to have resolved the argument, he would say, "Everything I said to you is because of your negative character traits. If you would have a more refined character, the entire argument would have been a peaceful discussion."*

*When I would hear this, I would immediately defend myself and tell him that he was really to blame. And he would go on for a long time trying to prove to me that I was to blame. Once aware of this pattern, I was resolved to let him say what he said without arguing. Not once did he ever agree with me when I argued that it was really his fault. And I didn't really lose out in any practical way from his saying that it was my fault. So even though I still feel that all our arguments are his fault, I don't try to enlighten him about this any more.*

## 34

# "I WISH
# I COULD REDO THAT."

MANY TIMES AFTER A QUARREL BOTH PEOPLE SAY TO themselves, "I wish I could redo that." In hindsight, it's easy to see how we could have spoken differently. It's easy to see that we could have spoken more concisely and to the point. It's easy to see that we didn't need to blame or speak condescendingly. It's easy to see that we shouldn't have made any insulting remarks.

Think about past situations when you spoke or acted in ways that now, when you are calm and thinking clearly, you wish you could redo.

While we can't go back to the past and actually redo situations, we can condition our brain in the present to be prepared to act with more wisdom, more patience, more compassion, more kindness, more respect.

Mentally redo situations of the past. See yourself thinking at your best. See yourself speaking at your best. And see yourself acting at your best.

"But this won't redo the past," some people complain. And they are right, it can't. But we can prepare ourselves for the future. Merely thinking about our negative words and actions might reinforce them. We didn't like them, but we are likely to repeat the same pattern, especially if we keep rerunning those same mental tapes and videos.

Now, in the present, mentally edit those tapes and videos. As you hear yourself speaking the way you wish you would have spoken in reality, and as you see yourself acting the way you wish you would have acted in reality, you will be conditioning your brain with the new and improved pattern. The more times you mentally run through the positive patterns, the stronger those improved patterns will become. And when you find yourself actually speaking and acting the way you would have wanted the first time around, you will know that you have made a lot of progress.

*I was irritated and upset and I was about to say something that would let the person know just how irritated and upset I was. But the thought came to me, "Later on when you calm down, you will regret your angry words. Later on you will wish that you had spoken with respect. Later on you won't be able to change what you said now. So right now speak and act in a way that you will feel good about later on." I had heard this mental program from my teacher, and I had repeated it over and over again in my mind just for occasions like the present. I pictured the smile on my teacher's face when I would report how I gained from our talk. And the great feelings of self-mastery outweighed any pleasure I might have gotten from releasing my anger by saying things I knew I would feel bad about later on.*

# 35

# IF IT DOESN'T WORK, DO SOMETHING ELSE

EOPLE WHO INTERACT EFFECTIVELY AND SUCCESSFULLY
with others have a rule: "If something you are saying or
doing doesn't work, do something else." Doesn't that sound
reasonable? If you were pushing a button and nothing happened, how many times would you have to push that same button to realize that pushing that button is not the way to get the
outcome you want? Eventually everyone will stop pushing that
button; it's just a question of how long the decision will take.

When it comes to arguing and quarreling, there are many
people who say the same ineffective or counterproductive
things over and over again. They hear and see that what they've
just said didn't make the situation better and could have made
it worse, yet they repeat those same verbal patterns again and
again. Habits are easy to repeat. But a habitual pattern that is
not doing what you want it to do is a message to "Say or do
something else."

Being aware of the rule of "If it doesn't work, do something
else" is valuable. Of course even without having this as a rule,
you know it. It's so obvious. But when you've seen intelligent

people repeat unresourceful patterns again and again, you come to realize the importance of having it stated as a communication rule.

When you look in a mirror, you have automatic feedback. You see right away whether you are reaching your goal or not. If you make a sad face, the mirror will reflect that sad face. If you make an angry face, the mirror will reflect an angry face. How many people will keep making a sad or angry face and hope to get a happy, smiling, joyful face in return? Not too many. At least not too many who are considered sane and normal. Everyone knows that if the way you are moving your facial muscles doesn't get you the vision of joy that you want, you need to change what you are doing with your facial muscles.

The same applies to interacting with another person. Change what you are saying and doing to get better results. If you are trying to get someone to speak to you with respect, and what you are saying and the way that you are saying it is not getting the results you want, say something else and change your tone of voice. When you keep applying this, it will be as obvious to you as moving your facial muscles to get a different look on your face when you look in a mirror.

*I kept telling someone who kept talking to me with disrespect, "Stop talking to me this way." Or, "The way you speak to me is rude and negative. Speak differently." But the person didn't speak any better to me. I was so used to talking this way that I didn't even think of trying a different approach. I just felt that this per-*

son was insensitive and stubborn, and nothing I would say could make a difference. Then I saw someone else interact with this person. This person began to speak with the same disrespect as he had spoken to me. But that new person said with a big smile, "You seem to me to be the type of person who has better patterns of speaking than this. Please speak to me the way that you would want me to speak to you." I was amazed to see the person I had difficulties with start speaking nicely to this person. I realized that my repetitive pattern hadn't worked and if I would try a pattern similar to the one I witnessed, I too would get better results.

## 36

# LEARN FROM THE SUCCESSES OF OTHERS

A WISE PERSON LEARNS FROM EVERYONE (*PIRKEI AVOS* 4:1). Every person you ever encounter will have had experience in resolving quarrels one way or another. Every young child has had quarrels with his parents, siblings, schoolmates, friends, and neighbors. Each person will have found ways to end quarrels.

If you want to gain expertise in avoiding and resolving quarrels, ask people you know, "What do you do to prevent quarrels?" and "What have you done to resolve a quarrel that you were involved in?" When asking this question, mention that you don't want to hear anything negative about any other person. You just want to know the patterns that this person has found effective in resolving disagreements and quarrels.

Even the most quarrelsome person around doesn't argue with everyone. There are some people with whom they get along. Find out how the people who get along with this person do it. You might even find it helpful to ask a person you find quarrelsome, "What enables you to get along well with other people?" Note: It's best not to say explicitly, "I find you quarrelsome and difficult to get along with. How do the people who get along with you do it?" Most likely this approach would not be appreciated. You might view this person as quarrelsome, but he might have a much more peaceful view of himself.

*At a wedding I was sitting near someone who had a reputation of being an expert at making peace between people. I asked him, "What did you do to learn how to make peace between people?"*

*"I basically did what you are doing now," he said to me. "Whenever I heard that someone was highly competent at making peace between people, I looked for opportunities to approach that person. 'What would you suggest I do when I try to make peace between people?' I would ask. When you ask this question to enough people, you can gain a lot of knowledge and insight."*

# 37

# PATIENCE
# AND PERSISTENCE

WHAT IF YOU TRY TO MAKE PEACE WITH SOMEONE who is angry at you and that person either refuses to speak to you or refuses to forgive you? Be patient and be willing to persevere.

How long must you be patient? As long as it takes. There is a well-known saying, "If at first you don't succeed, try, try again." Successful people are those who keep trying until they succeed.

The very fact that you are willing to call that person again and again, or are willing to write to that person again and again, gives that person a message that you are sincerely sorry for any wrongs that you have committed. You are conveying your inner feelings that this person is important to you and that you would like to have a peaceful relationship.

Most salespeople give up after one or two refusals. But the really successful salespeople know that it often takes five or more tries until someone will agree to buy what they are offering. Learn from them to be just as patient and persistent when it comes to making peace with someone.

The same applies to making peace between two other parties. When you first begin trying, the people might not be interested in what you have to say. But as you keep trying over and over again, you might come up with a successful formula.

Giving up is the only way to fail. As long as you keep trying, there is always a possibility that you will eventually succeed.

*A middle-aged man, who had finally made peace with someone who had refused to speak to him for two years, related, "I called that person up about once a week. He would say that he didn't want to talk to me, and I politely wished him well. I realized that I had made a mistake and caused him distress and I wanted to make amends for what I did. I viewed each telephone call as an opportunity to build up my own patience and perseverance 'muscles.' I was willing to call up weekly for as many weeks as it would take. I was resolved not to have any time limit. I felt a tremendous amount of relief when after approximately two years, my friend said to me, 'I am impressed with how long you have been trying. I forgive you for what you did wrong. I would like to renew our friendship.'"*

## 38

# LET THE OTHER PERSON EXPRESS HIS FEELINGS

THERE IS A SKILL THAT IS CONDUCIVE TO PEACE THAT IS one of the most difficult skills to master and, at the same time, one of the simplest skills to master. This is the skill of letting the other person express his feelings.

If someone angry at you expresses those angry thoughts and feelings, you will know where you stand and that person will let off steam. This process of self-expression enables the other person to become calmer. You gain from hearing the other person's issues and concerns.

This is a simple skill because you only need to remain silent and listen attentively. Listen to understand as objectively as you can. You've done this many times already in your life, and so this is a skill with which you have much experience. This is also a difficult skill because it can be highly distressful and painful to listen. This is difficult because it can take a lot of patience to listen to understand when you have an intense urge to express yourself. You want to disagree. You might want to show the other person that he is mistaken. Your own feelings can be hurt from before, and after listening to this person's emotionally-laden speech, your own emotions might be stirred up. The self-mastery and inner strength that it takes to listen attentively to understand helps you upgrade these qualities.

When you keep your focus on achieving your goal of creating peace and harmony, you will find it easier to allow the person to let off steam. Before that person does so, you won't be able to make progress. You are making a heroic step forward by mastering this skill.

When you are the person who has a need to express feelings, be very careful how you do so. Don't speak in such a way that the other person feels attacked. Rather, express your feelings in a way that enlightens the other person about how you experienced the situation, without causing him to become overly defensive. Expressing feelings in a blaming way is likely to cause a counterattack. Expressing feelings in a constructive way leads to more peaceful interactions.

*"I can't just let people go on and on expressing their feelings when they are wrong. I have to correct them."*

*This individual's constantly correcting others created many arguments that lasted for a much longer time than was really necessary.*

*"You'll save yourself a lot of time by letting the person speak his heart out," an experienced counselor told him. "And then you can resolve the quarrel. If you're interacting with someone who appreciates your corrections in the middle of his narrative and is willing to give them a fair hearing, then go ahead and make the corrections right away. But if the other person won't listen to what*

*you have to say until he expresses himself, view your patient listening as an act of courage and inner strength. This is a major reason why some people aren't able to discuss difficult matters in a quarrel without a mediator. A skillful mediator can enable both people to express themselves in a constructive manner and then move forward."*

## 39

# WHAT ARE THE REAL ISSUES?

MANY ARGUMENTS AND QUARRELS MIGHT APPEAR superficially to be about relatively trivial and inconsequential matters. But under the surface, subjectively important issues are what the argument is really about.

At times, they could be childhood issues. One's parents might have been highly critical of him, and the way this person is speaking now is reminiscent of those distressful criticisms. It could be that one had controlling siblings or siblings that said painful insults, and this person is reminding him of them. Realizing that this discussion in the present actually has nothing to do with what anyone has said or done in the past will help calm the stormy waters.

At times, one is feeling unsuccessful in an important area of one's life. And feeling put-down now adds to those painful feelings. Hence one might overreact. It's not the present discussion in itself that causes the reaction, it is the general feeling of lacking success that is the real issue.

A person might not feel confident enough about his intellect, and therefore the present argument is not really about whether or not a minor detail was correct. It's really about defending his intelligence.

A person might feel that he isn't assertive enough and others tend to take advantage of his softer personality, so now he feels a need to defend his right to have rights and therefore he overreacts.

Whenever you find yourself becoming intensely emotional about a topic of disagreement, ask yourself what your real issues actually are.

There are many possibilities about what the real issues could be. Thinking in this direction is likely to help you gain a proper perspective about what a specific argument means to you.

And just as you are likely to have underlying issues, the person you are arguing with is also likely to have underlying issues. Knowing what they are will be helpful in finding a resolution to the present argument.

*An expert peace-maker related: "Whenever I try to make peace between two parties, the question I try to answer for myself and for everyone involved is: 'What are the issues in your life that this specific argument brings up for you?' This is especially beneficial when the parties involved are family members who truly want to know what the other person is thinking and feeling. The smoke from the fire of arguments prevents both parties from seeing clearly. Getting both parties to articulate the underlying factors about why the present argument has such a strong emotional impact on them is an important first step. Self-understanding and understanding of the other person's reactions enables them to discuss the present conflict with mutual respect."*

## 40
# STAY ON TRACK

**I** AM A PERSON WHO CONSIDERS PEACEFUL INTERACTIONS *to be very important in my life. Yet with some people I find myself arguing and being unable to get along. I wanted to find out what was wrong with my present pattern and what new pattern would help me interact peacefully and harmoniously. It took me a while to view the situation from this perspective. I used to just put the blame on the other people. But this didn't give me any insight into what I could do for the sake of peace.*

*"I spoke to someone who was competent at recognizing present patterns and suggesting new ones. After asking questions to see what I was doing, he gave me the feedback that I needed. It was true I wanted peace and I always began by speaking pleasantly to others. But when I dealt with people who argued with me, I became irritated and annoyed. Instead of addressing their concerns, I took their comments and questions as personal attacks. Then my tone of voice and what I said became defensive. But I never did address the issues that were bothering the other person. So we didn't resolve anything.*

*"The new pattern I was taught was to remain calm and let the other person express their objections. Then I was to calmly answer those objections. My goal was that nothing anyone would say*

*would get me off track. Staying on track also enabled me to modify my original position if I saw that the points the other person made were valid."*

This fellow's experience is a pattern we need to model. The first step is to recognize your present pattern and find new patterns if the other patterns aren't conducive to working things out peacefully. You might find this pattern on your own, or you might need to consult someone who can pinpoint your present pattern and suggest a new one.

A common pattern that prevents harmonious interactions is getting off track because of the verbal challenges of the other person. Stay calm. Listen carefully to those challenges. Answer those that can be answered, and be willing to modify what you say and do.

If the other person speaks to you in an angry tone of voice, it's easy to get off track. If the other person speaks condescendingly or mockingly, it's easy to get off track. If the other person brings up points that are only tangentially related to the present discussion and he does so to push your buttons, it's easy to get off track. And even if you do get off track, be resilient. Come back to a centered place, focus on what you need to say,o and say it flowingly.

# 41
# SMALL STEPS AT A TIME

THERE CAN BE MAJOR BREAKTHROUGHS AND PEOPLE WHO have quarreled bitterly for a long time can resolve the quarrel in a relatively short time. The parties will go from being adversaries to being warm friends rather quickly. But don't count on it. Very often, progress towards making peace is a slow process.

A small step in the right direction will help you reach your destination eventually if you keep going. Knowing this, you can feel a sense of accomplishment if you make a situation better, even though there is still a long way to go.

People can react towards small steps in one of two basic patterns. One way is to think and feel, "The amount of progress we made is so tiny that it will take more patience than I have to have a real peace. I feel discouraged." The other attitude, the one that is recommended, is to think and feel, "We are on the path of peace. By consistently doing all that I can, I will be building up my character traits of patience and persistence. I know that if I keep going in this direction, I will succeed."

Appreciate each small step of progress, both when you are trying to make peace between two other people or when you yourself are involved in a quarrel. Let each bit of progress strengthen your sense of encouragement.

*I work hard trying to make peace between people. One of my biggest challenges is to influence people to have a sense of optimism even though there has been only slight progress. When I interact with two parties who were engaged in a conflict, I will point out each small step forward. Some people appreciate this, and realize that this is what's needed. But others tend to be pessimistic.*

*"The rate of our progress is not at all what I would like it to be," some will say. "And it's all because this other person is stubborn and arrogant. It's all his fault in the first place. I don't like the way you are praising him for his minor improvements. He still has a long way to go before the way he acts towards me is acceptable. If he doesn't make big changes and make them fast, I don't believe that we'll ever get anywhere."*

*I point out to people who say such things, "I can't guarantee you that the small steps forward will make the situation exactly the way you wish it would be. But I can guarantee that if we don't make these steps forward, we won't get anywhere. Blaming and attacking the other person is taking you both in the wrong direction. Please be patient. In the long run when you look back, you'll be happy that you were willing to take these small steps."*

# 42

# SETBACKS ARE PART OF THE PROCESS

W HEN YOU TRY TO MAKE PEACE, EITHER FOR yourself or between two other people, expect setbacks. They are part of the process.

Many people are happy, even excited, to make peace when they see steady progress. Even if progress is slow, they are patient. But they easily give up when faced with setbacks. One must realize that setbacks are an integral part of progress; they are just steps in the process. It's like climbing a mountain path. The path doesn't always go straight up. At times it goes around the right and at times it goes around the left, but the focus is on eventually getting to the destination. So, even if part of the path seems to be descending, it is a descent that leads to ascent. Setbacks, too, are getting you closer to where you want to end up.

People who give up after experiencing a setback are likely to be telling themselves, "I see that nothing I've done so far has made any difference whatsoever. It's not worth trying anymore. We're back to the beginning."

People who don't allow setbacks to stop them have the attitude, "Progress is always two steps forward and one step backward. The setback is only one step backward. The progress we make will eventually be successful. Of course, I would like to take two steps forward with no steps backward. But that's not how these things actually work."

Everyone experiences setbacks in important projects and ventures. When a project is valuable enough, after any setback you strengthen yourself and keep doing all that you can. Making peace for yourself or between other people is extremely valuable. Keep your focus on your goal and keep saying and doing what you can to create peace.

*I once heard an account of a lawyer who negotiated a peace settlement at a major company whose employees were on strike. An interviewer said, "This strike lasted a long time and many harsh and bitter words were said during this time. What enabled you to keep negotiating for so long, to allow you to reach this settlement?"*

*"I am paid according to the difficulty," he said. "If everyone agreed to my first round of trying, I wouldn't be making the kind of living that I am. I have a professional obligation to accomplish what I need to accomplish in as short a time as possible. But if there are many setbacks and it takes a long time, my fees are higher. This keeps me going as long as it will take."*

*People don't let setbacks stop them when they are being paid more because of those setbacks. The spiritual and emotional benefits of making peace can give us at least a similar motivation to overcome the disappointment of setbacks.*

# 43
# LEVELS OF APOLOGIES

APOLOGIES COME IN MANY FORMS. ON ONE SIDE THERE are apologies where the person sincerely feels strong distress for causing you distress. This is noticeable in his face, words, and tone of voice. The sincerity and depth of feeling are clear. On the other side are apologies that are as short as possible and have all the feeling of a solid rock.

A person might say, "I'm sorry if you think I might have offended you." The words, "I'm sorry," are certainly here, but the qualification of the second half of the sentence gives a message, "I personally don't think that I did anything wrong." At times, a person really didn't realize that he did anything wrong, but the sincerity of the apology is clear: The person really is sorry that you were distressed, just that he hadn't realized it.

The more a person loves and pursues peace, the more open he will be to accept apologies. When you have a strong will and desire for peace, anything at all that can be construed as an apology will be viewed as a great opportunity to begin to create a real peace.

Some people respond to apologies, "I see that you're sorry. But you're not sorry enough." Or, "You can't just say you're sorry and think that you can immediately have peace.'"

The ideal goal would be to master a consistently unequal policy. When you are on the receiving end of an apology, make it as easy as possible for the other person's apology to be accepted. Even if you would have preferred a more heartfelt apology, let any apology at all serve as a vehicle for creating an eventual real peace. And if you are the one apologizing, apologize over and over until the other party's needs are met.

Is this equal? It's definitely not equal, but it is elevating. Is this fair? When pursuing peace is a high priority, the fairness isn't the key question that you will consider. Rather, your focus will be on, "Will this approach lead to peace?" If it will, that's what will be important to you.

*A friend of mine was caused a lot of anguish by the actions of an insensitive person. I was standing nearby when that person approached him and said, "Yom Kippur is approaching. If I hurt you, will you forgive me?" My friend responded with an authentic smile, and said, "Of course. May you have a wonderful year."*

*"How could you respond so cheerfully?" I asked him.*

*"It took more inner effort than was apparent to you," he replied. "Spiritually and emotionally I want to let this go. So I applied all of my inner resources to accept his apology. The positive feelings I have caused by forgiving makes the effort well worthwhile."*

# 44

# FORGIVE!

FORGIVE! THIS IS AN EASY WORD TO SAY. IT CAN BE emotionally difficult to put into action.

Forgive! This is the first step towards making peace.

Forgive! This frees you from the emotional distress and psychosomatic problems caused by resentment, anger, and grudges.

Forgive! This enables you to be more serene and joyful.

Forgive! This clears your mind and enables you to think at your optimal level.

Forgive! This elevates you spiritually.

Forgive! Imagine what situation we would all be in if the Almighty wouldn't forgive us. The Almighty deals with us measure for measure. If we forgive the Almighty's children, the Almighty will forgive us.

*I was highly resentful towards a former friend who had taken advantage of my kindness towards him. I had given him a job, and then he had spoken against me to a number of people. I had a question about whether I should do another favor for him.*

*"This isn't really a question," my rabbi told me. "You should forgive him and as long as you won't lose out now, do him the favor."*

"But it's not so easy to just forgive him when he doesn't ask for my forgiveness," I complained.

"True," said my rabbi. "But just as when you do the kindness you become a better person, so too when you forgive you become a better person. The more difficult this is, the greater you become."

## 45

# KEEP ENTERING THE OTHER PERSON'S MIND

WHAT IS COMMUNICATION? SAYING SOMETHING TO another person for some purpose. Therefore, in every communication, the way the listener sees what you are saying, how he hears it, and how he feels about it are integral parts of your communication. As the communication principle states, "The meaning of your communication is the results you get."

Someone might build up his vocabulary to communicate better. Someone might practice his diction. Someone might practice conveying his feelings and emotions. Someone might practice writing what he wants to say and might consult a number of expert editors for their feedback. But still a crucial ingredient could be missing: The awareness of what is going on in the mind of the listener.

We don't have telepathy, so we can never be certain of what is going on in someone's mind unless he gives us feedback. This feedback might be direct and clear verbal statements, or this feedback might be subtle, nonverbal nuances. We should build up our skill at trying to enter the mind of the recipient of our communication. The more we practice, the better we'll become at this.

Keep imagining that you are listening to what you are saying from inside the mind of the person with whom you are communicating. Based on what you know about him, what do you think he is hearing? How is he reacting to what you are trying to convey? Are you accomplishing what you wanted to accomplish?

Even after doing this for a long time, we might not always be one hundred percent accurate. But at the very least, there are many things that we just won't say when we project ourselves into the listener's mind. Even a moment's projection would make it clear to us that certain ways of speaking are counterproductive and not in the interests of peace.

*I once met an excellent elementary school teacher who had a fabulous reputation for consistently bringing out the best in each pupil. "What is the key to your success?" I asked.*

*"I constantly see and hear everything I say from the minds of the children I speak to. 'What are they hearing?' I keep asking myself."*

*There was someone with whom I often had highly challenging conversations. Keeping this teacher's words in mind, I had one of the smoothest conversations ever the next time we interacted.*

## 46

# THE GREATNESS OF GOING AGAINST YOUR FEELINGS

*"I don't feel like making up with this person."*
*"I don't feel like asking forgiveness."*
*"I don't feel like forgiving."*
*"I don't feel that I want to speak with respect to this person."*
*"I don't feel like conquering my anger."*

OUR FEELINGS HAVE A STRONG INFLUENCE ON OUR behavior. When we don't feel like doing something, we tend not to do it. The goal is to do what is right, whether or not we feel like it. The goal is to refrain from saying or doing things that are wrong, even if we feel like doing them.

There is greatness in acting in elevated ways that go against the way we feel like speaking or acting. "Who is a mighty person? The one who conquers his evil inclination" (*Pirkei Avos* 4:1).

"But what if I feel the way I do because deep within I know that it will be potentially harmful and dangerous to be friendly with a specific person?" That's different. The question we need to answer is: "What do I really think is the right thing to do based on all I know about this other person and myself?" If you intuitively feel that it would be a mistake to make peace with someone, that's very different from situations when you know that you should make peace but just don't feel like doing it.

*I used to think that if I didn't feel like doing something that's a good enough excuse for not doing it. What changed my mind was a time when I was experiencing a distressful problem and asked a few people to help me out. Basically, each one said that they didn't feel like helping me. They worded it with a little more sophistication than that, but this was essentially what they were saying. I was helped out by someone who did feel like helping me, and I was extremely grateful. But this gave me the impetus to make a resolution that if something was the right thing to do, I would access the inner strength to do it, whether or not I felt like doing it.*

## 47
# ACT AS IF IN A PLAY

A T TIMES WE WOULD LIKE TO ACT IN A MORE FRIENDLY, cheerful, kind, elevated, spiritual, transcendent way towards someone but we feel stuck. We feel that we are not on the level to do this. We feel too hurt. We might even feel that this would be impossible for us.

There is a way to add new patterns of speech and behavior to your repertoire. Act as if you were in a play. Imagine that you were being paid a tremendous amount of money to play the role of a certain friendly, cheerful, kind, elevated, spiritual, transcendent person. You will be paid so much money for doing this that you will be wealthy beyond your wildest dreams. Playing this role well will give you opportunities to raise money for great charitable institutions. It will open doors for you that would have been closed before. Playing this role well will give you opportunities that seemed impossible for you before. So now you are totally motivated. You are even enthusiastic about playing this role.

Mentally imagine how you will speak in this role of a person who is friendly, cheerful, kind, elevated, spiritual, and transcendent. Imagine how you will act. Run this through your mind over and over again. Your brain is fast and you can do this hundreds of times in a relatively short time.

As you mentally see yourself in the role of someone who is friendly, cheerful, kind, elevated, spiritual, and transcendent, think the thoughts that someone would think if he were this way naturally. Even some of these thoughts will be beneficial.

Now you will be ready to put your role-playing into action when it really counts. When you interact with a person you find challenging, it's time for you to play your role. Now is the time to master this role. Every time you practice, you will be gaining expertise. The more difficult it is for you to do this, the greater you become because of it. Professional actors have it relatively easy. They aren't dealing with real-life adversaries. You are. They have a coach to direct them. You are your own coach. They have a friendly audience when they do well. Even when you do well, your audience might still be negative and adversarial. So your performance is all the more praiseworthy.

By role-playing you will be able to act in more elevated ways than you felt you could before. By role-playing you create this way of being as your authentic character. By role-playing you are likely to influence the other person to react so much better towards you.

And with an additional awareness, your performance takes on a greater dimension. You have the Almighty, your Father, your King, as your audience who is wishing you success. Your royal performance will be eternally rewarded.

*It was suggested to me to act better towards someone when I felt that it would be impossible for me to do so. When I argued that this just wasn't me, I was told, "Begin by acting this way as if in a play, in order to eventually make this your inner reality."*

*"I like to be sincere and authentic. I don't go for this acting stuff," I argued.*

*"It's wonderful to be sincerely and authentically a person with elevated character. And if you aren't naturally this way, you are making a choice. Should you speak and act in ways that are negative and counterproductive just because that is the way you have been before? Or should you elevate yourself by acting in more elevated ways? Our mission in this world is to elevate ourselves. We need to work on it. Don't wait until you spontaneously become a more elevated person to speak and act better. Since this is so valuable, it makes sense to act this way. This is authentically who you want to be."*

*This made sense to me. And in actuality I found it much easier than I had thought. The power of this approach has enhanced my life in all areas.*

# 48

# EXPECT PEOPLE TO THINK DIFFERENTLY

WOULDN'T IT BE WONDERFUL IF EVERYONE would see things the way we do? If everyone would have the same opinions that we do? If everyone would value what we value? If everyone would agree that what we consider to be a high priority would be their highest priority also? If everyone we care about would agree with our decisions and choices?

But that's not the way that this world works. "Just as no two people look exactly alike, so too, no two people think exactly alike," said the Sages. And the Kotzker Rebbe commented, "Just as it doesn't bother you that no one else looks exactly like you, so too, it shouldn't bother you that no one else will think exactly like you." Since this is the reality of the world, it makes sense to accept it.

Discuss points of disagreement. You might try to convince someone else that your opinions, perspectives, values, priorities, decisions, and choices are correct, and the intelligent thing for them to do would be to agree with you. Do this peacefully. As one scholar pointed out to another who raised his voice during a disagreement, "Even if you raise your voice and state your opinion in the loudest voice possible, you still haven't proven your point."

It can be exasperating when you feel certain that your view is correct and the other person is totally wrong but doesn't agree to see it your way. This is the time to build up your ability to stay calm and focused even during challenging moments.

When you expect everyone to think the way you do, you'll become frustrated more frequently. When you realize that everyone thinks differently, you'll realize that diverse opinions and perspectives are the norm. This makes it easier to handle disagreements.

*I met someone who had strong views on many subjects but always discussed them with an inner calm. I asked him, "Doesn't it bother you that others disagree with your opinions and ways of viewing things?"*

*"Yes, it does," he replied.*

*"But you don't react very emotionally about their not seeing things your way," I said.*

*"I care but I don't care too much," he said. "If they will disagree I can choose to try to get them to see the validity of my thoughts. And I choose to state my positions clearly and bring logical arguments and proofs that I am correct. But I know that I also have a choice whether to stay inwardly calm or to become irritated, upset, and even angry. Since this is my choice, I choose inner calm. This is healthier for me: It helps me get along more peace-*

*fully with others, and it makes it easier for me to express myself in a way that might possibly win the other person over. I see remaining calm as a totally beneficial way of being, without any negative side effects. Just as I choose to see things the way that I think is correct, so too I choose to remain emotionally calm."*

# 49

# KNOW THAT
# YOU DON'T KNOW

W HAT EXACTLY IS GOING ON IN THE MIND OF THE person with whom you are quarreling? Know that you don't know. One thing that is absolutely certain is that this person is not thinking the exact same thing that you are. He certainly sees things differently.

Even in a relatively simple situation, such as two people entering a wedding hall at the same time, no two people will think the exact same thoughts. There are many patterns from which to choose, and even people with similar patterns will have many variations. Some will be thinking, "I wish the young couple well. I hope that they will have a harmonious life." Some will be thinking, "I hope that I look good." Some will be thinking, "I'm concerned whether I will have an enjoyable time." Some will be thinking, "I hope that the food will taste good." Some will be thinking, "I wonder which band they will have." Some will be thinking, "I love being part of a happy crowd." Some will be thinking, "I can't stand all this noise, and seeing all these people at one time makes me nervous." Some will be thinking, "I have to rush out as soon as possible for an important appointment."

Some will be thinking, "They didn't invite me to the meal. I'm very disappointed." Some will be thinking, "I'm glad that I wasn't invited for the meal. I'm on a diet." Some will be thinking, "There is someone I like talking to. I'll approach him and we'll have an enjoyable conversation." Some will be thinking, "No one is coming over to talk to me. I feel lonely in this crowd." Some will be thinking, "I choose the experience I will have here and I will choose a growth experience."

Many people will attend a wedding, and each one has a unique experience. And each person who is involved in a quarrel will have a unique experience. You might think it's obvious that they way you see things is the way they really are, and that the other person probably realizes this but doesn't have the inner strength to acknowledge it. The other person might be thinking in a similar pattern, with the roles being reversed.

When you think you know something that you don't, you will be making errors without realizing it. When you realize that you don't know all that is going on in someone's mind, you take an approach that is more research oriented. Your goal is to understand the other person better. If the other person knows that he doesn't know what is going on in your mind and also takes a research approach, you both have a better chance of working out a peaceful resolution.

*"I know exactly what this person is thinking and why he is thinking that," the angry participant of a quarrel stated.*

*"What do you think he is thinking?" he was asked.*

*"He thinks that I am someone he can use as his punching bag. He knows he is hurting me with what he says and he is doing it anyway," was the angry reply.*

*When the other party was asked about what he was thinking, he said, "I don't understand why this person is always so angry at me. I just want him to treat me with normal respect. I'm not asking for much. I always have to defend myself against his attacks. He knows how much he is hurting me and he does it anyway."*

*The person who shared this pattern was asked if he was usually successful in getting each one to understand what the other one was really thinking. He responded that sometimes he is and sometimes he isn't. Some people are relieved to hear that the other person doesn't really want to cause them pain. Others argue, "Even if he says that he doesn't want to cause me pain, actions speak louder than words. I know that he wants to cause me distress."*

*"When I can influence such individuals to realize that they can't possibly read the other person's mind and that it's in their best interests to assume that the person doesn't have negative intentions, I am able to make peace between them," he told me.*

## 50

# STATING WHAT
# YOU REALLY FEEL

W HEN PEOPLE QUARREL, SOME SAY THINGS THAT clearly make things worse. When asked about why they are doing this, some reply, "I think it's important to always say what I really feel. I'm just being authentic when I tell this person how awful I think he is."

Stating what you really feel can be a beautiful thing when you are full of unconditional love and kindness and compassion and encouragement and optimism and sincere good will. Stating what one really feels can be counterproductive when someone is full of hatred and anger and animosity and resentment and pessimism and sincere bad will.

What you really feel at a given moment is based on the reality of that moment. When you focus on saying and doing things to improve a relationship, the positive things you say and do will have a positive influence on the other person. And then when that person speaks to you in a better way and treats you with greater respect, those authentic negative feelings will melt away. Since what you feel is always temporary, don't say negative things that might be remembered and obsessed about for a long time to come.

The goal of making peace is a much higher priority than expressing feelings of negativity in a way that will create friction, anger, and hatred. Make it your goal to increase your feelings of unconditional love and kindness and compassion and encouragement and optimism and sincere good will so that you will not have a problem with expressing your true feelings when they are appropriate.

*Someone went for counseling and was told that it's not good for his emotional health to keep in his negative feelings. He was resolved to tell anyone who annoyed him how angry he felt. When this person reported to the counselor how he was expressing his anger, the counselor encouraged this pattern. "Keep it up. Get in touch with your real feelings. Let people know when you hate what they did, when you feel resentment, when you are angry at them." Being an obedient sort of chap this fellow followed the doctor's orders. The results were disastrous. He got into more fights in just two weeks than he had in the previous thirty years. His feelings of anger and resentment kept growing and the new quarrels he got into were harming him greatly. I told this person to ask the counselor whose theories he was following. The counselor told him, and I told him to read a biography of that person's life. He did and found out that the person whose theories they were following was divorced a couple of times, had children who felt so negatively towards him that they didn't invite him to their weddings, and that the only people who did get along with him were those who followed him blindly. This was certainly not the pattern he wanted to emulate.*

# 51

# SEEING THE PAIN OF THE OTHER

WHEN PEOPLE ARE IN EMOTIONAL PAIN, THEY TEND to speak and act in ways that sound angry and aggressive. And if you, too, are in emotional pain, you are likely to speak to the other person in ways that he will perceive as angry and aggressive. Each person adds to the emotional pain of the other, and the distress of everyone involved keeps increasing.

When you are calm, it's easier to see the emotional pain of others. That is when you can build up your attribute of compassion. The goal is to have so much compassion that even when you personally are experiencing emotional pain, you are able to be sensitive to the emotional pain of the person with whom you are interacting.

Coming from a place of compassion, you will be able to address the thoughts and feelings of the other person in a way that alleviates his distress. Then he is more likely to speak and act more sensibly and reasonably towards you.

An issue that many people have when they quarrel is, "Why should I be sensitive to his pain? He's not sensitive to my pain! What's more, he is the cause of my pain."

Being compassionate is an elevated character trait. Every time you speak and act compassionately, you are building your own character. Don't allow someone else's limitations to prevent you from growing to be all that you can be.

*There was someone with whom I had a business connection for quite a long time. We always got along smoothly. I was taken by surprise one day when he spoke to me in a very agitated manner. There were some details in our latest deal that didn't work out as planned. This person blamed me in an attacking way. Fortunately, I was aware that if I would remain centered and focused, we would be able to work things out. I realized that this person must have been in a lot of pain to speak to me the way he did. A few hours later, he called me up and apologized for the way he had spoken.*

*"My anger wasn't really because of anything you did or said. I was going through a rough time. That's why I spoke the way I did," he said with relief that I had handled it well.*

*Our future business association was mutually beneficial. I'm very glad I was able to maintain a calm, understanding state.*

## 52
# IT'S JUST A TEST

"**E**VERYTHING IN THIS WORLD IS JUST A TEST." THIS often-quoted statement is from the first chapter of Rabbi Moshe Chaim Luzzatto's "Path of the Just." When you view every challenge to peace as a test, you will find it much easier to pass the test.

Imagine that you were told in advance, "This fellow is trying to test you, to see if he can get you involved in an angry quarrel." Now you are mentally prepared. It wouldn't be that difficult to control your reactions, would it?

Getting high marks on tests gives one a great feeling. Conversely, failing a test, even one that isn't that important, creates bad feelings (unless someone is a master at positive reframing). All the more so, does failing an important test.

Your character is being tested in this world over and over again. That's why you are here. Right now, mentally prepare yourself to pass with flying colors the tests that come your way.

*There was a specific person in my life who frequently pushed my anger buttons. Even when I didn't become angry, I felt highly frustrated. I am embarrassed to say that at times I completely lost it and shouted. I tried to control my reactions. But again and again I wasn't satisfied with the way I responded.*

*I asked someone I respected what to do to gain greater self-mastery.*

*"View your encounters with him as a game. In this game your skill will be tested over and over again. Look forward to the opportunities to pass the tests that come your way."*

*I can't say that this game was tremendous fun, but I did find myself improving greatly.*

# 53
# FACIAL EXPRESSIONS

F ACES GIVE MESSAGES. WHEN YOU GREET SOMEONE, YOUR face might reflect the thoughts, "I am happy to see you," and "I sincerely wish you well." Faces can also give messages that are the opposite: messages that one feels displeased with another person, that one is apprehensive or nervous, that one is blaming and critical.

When two people were involved in a previous quarrel, and now one person greets the other with a sincerely positive facial expression, that positive non-verbal message might be more helpful than any words that could be spoken. Just moving your muscles is insufficient to convey a totally positive message: For this you need to think thoughts of mental blessings. Then your face automatically gives a positive message. Your conscious mind can't force all of your muscles to do this. Your inner mind does this spontaneously when the conditions of your thoughts are conducive to this reaction.

If you feel that your negative thoughts about someone will cause your face to give that person a negative message and create negativity between the two of you, practice thinking positive thoughts about that person in front of a mirror. The feedback reflected in your mirror will show you what your face is expressing. This feedback will make it easier for you to upgrade the messages that you are conveying.

*I had just heard about a serious injury that someone I cared about suffered, and I was deeply worried about this person's welfare. I had to pick up a number of items from our local grocery store, and the entire time what was uppermost in my mind was my concern for the condition of my friend. Later that day I received a telephone call. "Did I say or do anything that offended you?" the caller asked me.*

*"Not in the least," I said with surprise. "Why do you think so?"*

*"Because this morning I passed you by in the store and the look on your face gave me the feeling that you feel negatively about me."*

*"I'm so sorry that I gave you a reason to think that way," I said. "The look on my face had nothing to do with you or anyone else that I met today. It was just because I was concerned about the injury of a friend of mine. I thank you for pointing this out."*

## 54

# RESPECT EACH PERSON'S POTENTIAL

THE WAY THAT SOMEONE IS RIGHT NOW IS A REFLECTION OF his history until this moment. At this very moment, he can make new choices about what he will say and do. We human beings can always make wiser, more elevated choices of words and actions.

Respect the potential of each human being with whom you interact. Believe in this person's ability to speak and act in ways that will enable both of you to interact harmoniously. Will this guarantee that everyone will be all that they can be? Of course not. But your belief in this person's potential to speak and act in ways that are friendly, kind, reasonable, fair, considerate, compassionate, and wise will have a higher probability of eliciting these patterns than if you didn't believe in this potential.

Some people are experts at bringing out the best in others. A common denominator in those who have gained this expertise is their belief in the potential of those they influence.

The way you view any other person is only one choice out of a multitude of possible ways of viewing him. Those who tend to view people in a negative light often feel that those who see people in a positive light are naïve and often mistaken. But the future is always unknown. So whatever anyone will project about the future verbal and behavioral patterns of someone else is only a guess. By guessing on the side of merit when this is a sensible thing to do, you are likely to be influential in making your projection a reality. Thinking with this pattern will help you get along peacefully with more people.

*"You'll never amount to anything," I was told as a high school student in many ways by different teachers. To say that I was unmotivated was to put it kindly. I didn't study, didn't pay attention in class, and got into frequent fights with other students. I was considered argumentative and quarrelsome. My constant sense of frustration was manifested in the way I spoke to and treated others. After high school, however, I met a mentor who believed in my hidden talents and the potential I had by developing my mind. A number of successes had me convinced that my present mentor was right and those who had written me off were wrong.*

*One of the greatest moments in my life was when I met my principal after he retired, and he told me, "You are now considered brilliant by all who know you, and you are a pleasure to deal with. I apologize to you for not believing in you when you were in my school. I wonder how many other students would have blossomed if we would have realized all that they could be and do."*

# 55

# WHAT DO YOU BOTH REALLY WANT?

O N THE BEHAVIORAL LEVEL, TWO PEOPLE MIGHT BE in conflict. But on the intentional level they might find it relatively easy to find ways to satisfy the needs of what they really want. Satisfy what two people really want and they can interact peacefully and harmoniously.

A husband and wife might argue and quarrel about where to go on a vacation. One might want to go to a peaceful cabin near a lake. The other might want to visit a certain city where they have a number of relatives. If they keep focusing on the behavior, where they want to go, they are likely to keep quarreling. If the real needs are focused on, visiting the relatives or finding a peaceful and calm place, they are more likely to find a way to meet both parties' needs. And they might decide to go to place "A" now and to place "B" next time.

Two business partners might argue about whether to expand or to consolidate. They might quarrel heatedly. Searching for what they really want, you will find that one wants to make more profits by preventing risk, and the other wants more profit by increasing business. Going further into what they want, both parties might consider it important that their opinions be given a fair hearing by the other. When this is the case, when each person listens carefully to understand the other's position, and gives verbal feedback of this understanding, the two people will find it easier to reach an acceptable solution.

Please note: When you ask someone, "What do you want?" the first answer might only address the surface position. By asking questions such as, "What do you really want?" you are likely to get answers that will be dealing with root issues. Resolving these will take you further down the path of peace.

*A husband and wife got into frequent quarrels. A basic theme that often repeated itself was that the husband kept telling the wife that she was shouting way too much, and the wife argued that she wasn't shouting and didn't like to be criticized for something she wasn't doing.*

*The person with whom they spoke asked a number of questions and found that the husband had a highly sensitive hearing ability. Even relatively low noise sounded loud to him. The wife, on the other hand, was a bit hard of hearing.*

*What did they really want? The wife didn't mind being told to speak in a quieter tone of voice, but she wanted to be spoken to respectfully. The husband accepted the idea that his wife wasn't at fault for speaking louder than he liked, and he agreed to suggest in a more friendly manner that she speak more softly. They both got what they really wanted. The wife felt she was being respected, and the husband was spoken to in a tone of voice that was more pleasant.*

# 56

# CHANGE, RATHER THAN HIDE, NEGATIVE FEELINGS

I F YOU DISLIKE SOMEONE, YOUR FACIAL EXPRESSION, TONE OF voice, and body language will convey this non-verbal message. Even if you try to hide it, it's almost inevitable that some aspects of this negativity will be manifest.

So what should you do if you don't like someone? Work on liking him.

Rabbi Noah Weinberg, dean of Aish HaTorah, frequently says, "Love is the pleasure of seeing virtue. Master the ability to see many positive qualities in each person."

Mentally focus on something positive when interacting with someone you find challenging. Even if this person has only a spark of a positive quality, build up your appreciation to such an extent that you actually respect this person for having that quality.

One way to create a positive feeling is to think of someone whom you respect and like. Then take those feelings and channel them towards this challenging person.

Another way to access positive feelings is to imagine that you are a world-class actor whose role it is to be someone who has totally mastered a sincere love of humanity. In the role you play, you feel authentic positive feelings towards even the most challenging people. Practice this when you are alone. Look into a mirror and see this reflected back at you. Visualize this before you go to sleep and when you wake up in the morning. As you mentally replay this over and over again and you act this way out in the real world, it eventually becomes your actual inner reality. And even if it doesn't, you have done all that you can do. This will certainly have an elevating effect on you and your life.

*"I have to be real with my feelings. If I dislike someone, that's my true feelings. I don't want to fake it until I make it, or anything like that,"* I said to the counselor who was trying to tell me to change my feelings towards someone.

*"Of course you should be true to yourself and recognize your present reality,"* he replied. *"This doesn't contradict the value of learning the skill of mastering your feelings. Just because you feel some way one moment doesn't necessarily mean that you have to keep feeling that way. We all have a stream of consciousness that keeps flowing along. One moment we think thoughts and visualize imagery that put us into one state, and at another moment we think thoughts and visualize imagery that put us into a very different state. As you master the ability to think thoughts conducive to respecting and appreciating the strengths and virtues of people, you will find that you authentically feel much more positively about them. Keep visualizing yourself feeling positively towards this person and this will eventually become your internalized reality."*

# 57
# TIMING IS CRUCIAL

I F YOU TRY TO APPROACH SOMEONE TO MAKE PEACE, THE timing of your approach will make a major difference. The same will apply to making peace between two parties when you were not at all involved in their quarrel.

When someone is in the midst of intense, angry feelings, he usually won't be open to listening to what another person will try to tell him. After he calms down, he is likely to be more reasonable. So it is usually wise to wait for the anger to subside.

With a quarrel or feud that has lasted a long time, when one party is in an especially joyful and celebratory state, he might be more open to hearing ideas about making peace. His positive state will often be conducive to forgiving the other party and taking the initiative to make peace.

In some instances the timing could be ripe for peace when there are challenging events in a person's life or challenges for the larger community.

Timing could also be right around Rosh Hashanah and Yom Kippur. These are times of introspection and repentance. We want the Almighty to forgive us, so we are more open to forgiving others. The timing might be right around Purim or Passover. These are days of celebration that are conducive to forgiveness. The timing might be right around the fast day of Tisha B'Av, which commemorates the destruction of the Temple, which was destroyed because of unwarranted hatred.

There are many factors that might make a specific timing conducive to accomplishing what wasn't accomplished before. When you look for opportunities for peace, you might find them.

*Rabbi Refael of Bershid was once visiting a certain town. On Tisha B'Av (the fast of the ninth day of the month of Av, which commemorates the destruction of the Holy Temple) he was informed of a bitter feud between two groups, and was asked to serve as mediator.*

*"We assume, however, that you will not want to hear the two sides until tomorrow, since today is a fast day," they told him.*

*"On the contrary," responded Rabbi Refael. "The destruction of the Temple was caused by unwarranted hatred* (Talmud, Yoma 9b). *What is more appropriate than trying to promote peace and brotherhood on this day?"* (Midrash Pinchos, *p. 33b*)

## 58

# IF YOU KNEW YOU WOULD SUCCEED

IF YOU HAD A ONE HUNDRED PERCENT GUARANTEE THAT IF you tried to make peace with someone you would be successful, with whom would you make peace?

Let this be your guide to making a goal. Right now this might seem like dreaming an impossible dream, but since human beings make new choices all the time, perhaps the person with whom you would like to make peace will decide to make new choices about how he will speak and act towards you.

Visualize yourself speaking to that person in a peaceful way. Visualize that person reacting towards you in a positive way. Be dedicated to making this your reality.

Allow yourself to imagine that you have a guarantee that you will succeed in making peace between two people or two groups who presently aren't getting along well with each other. Which person or groups would you choose? See what you can do in reality to make progress on this dream. If you feel that you personally can't accomplish this peace, think of someone else who might be able to do so.

*There was someone with whom I had a quarrel, and deep down I strongly wanted to make peace with him. I tried to analyze what stopped me and what quality would help me approach this person. The one word that came to my mind was "courage." I felt I lacked the courage to approach this individual. I was afraid of how he would react towards me. Then I asked myself, "If I knew that I couldn't fail, what would I do?" The answer was simple. I would approach him as soon as I could. Then I realized that if I intensified my state of courage, I could do it. Thinking about how upgraded courage would empower me made me realize that this is the same power that I would feel if I were guaranteed success. Then I would feel comfortable approaching the people I needed to approach, and I would be able to speak smoothly. I kept repeating the word "courage" to myself over and over again. My renewed friendship with my former adversary is my proof to the effectiveness of this method.*

## 59

# IF IT WON'T HELP, DON'T START AN AVOIDABLE QUARREL

S IT WORTH GETTING INTO QUARRELS EVERY TIME YOU ARE right and the other person is wrong? Certainly not! When there is a friendly exchange of diverse ideas, different opinions and perspectives are the topics of interesting discussion. But angry quarrels over trivial matters that get nowhere are a waste of precious time and energy.

"But I am right," is the fighting cry that has led many people into lose-lose battles. If it won't be helpful and beneficial to sustain a heated exchange, find better ways to spend your time.

Since you feel that you are right, you might feel that it is very important for you to express your thoughts. Do so in a mutually respectful manner. Then stop. "But I still haven't convinced the other person that I am right. So how can I stop?" many tell themselves. So how many repetitions do you feel are necessary until you feel it is wiser to stop, even though the other person is still unconvinced? Answering this question will save you a lot of wasted time.

*I interviewed an experienced family counselor who worked with countless families over the years.*

*"What do you consider to be the most prevalent mistake that family members make?" I asked him. "And how do you resolve it?"*

*"There's a common pattern that quarreling family members often repeat," he said. "They argue and quarrel over the same issues over and over again. They know from experience that their quarreling won't be beneficial. They have seen over and over again that the way they speak to the other person doesn't bring them closer to a resolution. Yet they repeat the pattern again and again. I've said many times, 'You know that arguing over this isn't helpful, why don't you just let it go?' and I'm often told, 'I can't refrain from commenting on this.' But the reality is that they do have the ability to refrain from commenting. All they have to do is not comment. It's as simple as that. But I acknowledge that it's not easy for them. Nevertheless, they would be wise to choose not to comment when the comment won't be helpful and will make things worse. Those who follow my advice – not to comment when comments won't help – save themselves a lot of distress."*

# 60

# FIND HUMOR
# IN THINGS THAT USED
# TO GET YOU UPSET

P EOPLE WHO HABITUALLY FIND HUMOR IN EVENTS, situations, and occurrences can find something to enjoy in challenging situations. Be careful not to laugh at another person, but inwardly find the humor. This is especially important when you are in the midst of a quarrel. If appropriate, share it with the other person if you feel that he, too, will find it humorous.

Learn from positive role models. Don't copy the patterns of those who make fun of others. Rather, emulate those who modestly and confidently mock themselves.

One aspect of humor is laughing when something is ridiculous or incongruous. Building up the importance of some trivial matter and wasting precious time and energy over a ridiculous quarrel has an element of humor. The outcome of quarrels is often too serious to be considered a laughing matter. But if you nip a potential quarrel in the bud, you both can laugh before a heated argument builds up.

"Just laugh." This is a piece of advice that can be useful if someone tries to make fun of you and isn't someone who will stop even when you say you find it distressing. Instead of quarreling, respond by laughing.

If the other person asks, "What's so funny?" you might reply, "My brain associates potentially irritating comments with my laughing state. I see that this prevents me from getting angry. Try it yourself. You'll see that laughing is a lot more enjoyable than getting angry or quarreling."

*I witnessed someone defuse a potentially explosive situation by interrupting two people's counterproductive interaction. Two people were just beginning to quarrel, and a third person said, "Wait a minute. I need a favor. I'm looking for something funny to say at the start of a speech I need to give. Did anyone here ever hear a joke they found funny?" The potential combatants stopped and someone else who was present related a joke that made everyone laugh. In their laughing state, the would-be quarrelers never did build up that potential quarrel.*

# 61

# DEFENSIVE OR AGGRESSIVE?

THERE IS A VERY COMMON PATTERN WITH QUARRELS. Both parties in the quarrel often view themselves as "just being defensive." They are feeling hurt or attacked and are just saying things to defend themselves. And both parties view the other as being the one who is aggressive.

If someone tries to point this out to them, they both react, "It's quite obvious to anyone who is open to seeing reality that I am clearly only reacting to his aggressiveness. Listen to what he says. Listen to his tone of voice. Observe his facial expression and body language."

So what is the reality? The reality from the outside is often exactly the way the first paragraph describes it: We tend to see ourselves as only reacting to the way that the other person is treating us, and the other person sees himself as only reacting to the way that we are treating him.

It could be true that one person is really much more aggressive than the other, but that person might not view himself in that light. When this is so, insisting that he was more aggressive usually won't be successful in calming the situation.

One of the best ways to handle this is to acknowledge to the other person, "I understand that from your viewpoint I am the aggressive one and you are just trying to defend yourself. But I don't intend to be aggressive. I am only trying to defend myself." When both parties acknowledge this to the other, they are often on the road to finding a solution.

If the other person views you as being aggressive even though you don't, apologize. "I didn't mean to be aggressive towards you. I'm sorry that I spoke or acted in the way that I did."

*"He always starts the quarrels," I used to say. "He has this angry expression and his tone of voice is accusatory." I believed that he was just lying when he kept accusing me of starting the quarrels. "You don't see the way your face looks in these situations," he said to me. "You don't hear the way you sound." We asked an outside observer to give us feedback.*

*"You are both partially correct," he told us. "Give up the quest to find out who is more aggressive. View yourselves as partners in harmonious communication. Put your main emphasis on controlling what you say and how you say it. When you work on your half in such a situation and are successful in mastering the way you speak and act, the other person will no longer feel a need to be defensive. With patience this will improve the entire situation.'*

*He concluded, "My suggestion is for both of you to view the other person's pattern as a reaction to your pattern. This will strengthen your resolve to speak and act in ways that will create peace."*

*Following his advice was a turning point in my life.*

# 62

# "WHAT WOULD HAPPEN IF...?"

THERE IS A POWERFUL TOOL THAT MANY PEOPLE USE TO change the focus and state of people who are angry or resentful: questions that begin with, "What would happen if...?"

Every question changes a person's focus and state. Imagine being asked these questions: "What are your favorite childhood memories?" "What music do you like to listen to?" "What books have you enjoyed reading?" "What character trait would you like to keep on developing?" As you think of answers, your focus will be channeled in the direction suggested by the question.

Utilize this power of questions to help people access positive, resourceful states and to overcome unresourceful states. If someone is upset or angry at something you have said or done, you can ask, "What would happen if we worked this out in a way that is satisfactory for you?" "What would happen if I would make amends?" "What would happen if I were totally committed not to say or do anything that would cause you distress?"

When you want to make peace between two other people, these forms of questions can be very helpful. Approach each person and ask, "What would happen if the other person were sorry that he caused you distress and would speak and act in ways that were mutually respectful and beneficial?"

You can ask yourself, "What would happen if I mastered the ability to bring out the best in other people?"

*"There is nothing anyone could say to me that would make me want to make peace with this person," the irate adversary stated with intensity.*

*Someone who heard this felt a need to take on the challenge. He reacted with a polarity to statements that essentially said, "Nothing can be done." This brought out his creativity and he would try to think of creative possibilities.*

*He waited a couple of days and then asked this person, "What would happen if our forefather Abraham came to you in a dream and said to you, 'My beloved grandchild, please make peace with this other grandchild of mine. You will gain much by doing so, and will lose out a lot by not doing so. You'll be surprised by how much you'll benefit. The very fact that you said you won't make peace makes you even greater for pursuing peace.' Wouldn't you consider making peace with him if you felt the dream were conveying the truth to you?"*

*"I guess I would have to consider it," he said reluctantly.*

*The person who elicited this response knew that the most important first step was already taken.*

# 63

# "IF I CAN SHOW YOU A BETTER WAY...?"

THERE IS AN EFFECTIVE TECHNIQUE FOR RESOLVING ISSUES that cause quarrels and it goes like this:

Ask, "What is the main factor behind your position?" After the person tells you the main factor, you can ask, "If I can show you a better way to obtain the outcome you want, would that resolve the issue for you?"

The answer won't always be positive, but when it is, and you can satisfactorily show the other person an alternative way to get what he wants, the present quarrel will be resolved.

This approach helps you deal with the underlying theme that is bothering the other person. Used properly, this will be a win-win approach.

Let's see a few examples. Imagine someone is raising his voice and screaming at you. Calmly and politely say, "Could I ask you a question? What is the main factor causing you to speak to me this way?" The person then says, "Because only if I speak to you this way will you listen to me and understand that this is important to me." Then you can say, "If I can show you another, more effective, way to get me to listen and to see that this is important to you, would you be willing to try it out?" Most people will say, "Yes." Then suggest a more preferable way this person can speak to you.

Suppose two partners are quarreling about what approach to use in their business. If one of the partners wants to settle the issue peacefully, he can ask, "What is the main factor behind your position?" The partner is likely to say, "Because I want us to make a bigger profit." Then the person can ask, "If I can show you what we can do to make a bigger profit, would you be willing to consult an unbiased expert with me to ask his opinion on what approach will make the biggest profit, taking the risk factor into consideration?"

If religious issues are the basis of the quarrel, you can ask, "What is the main factor behind your position?" The person might say, "I want to make certain to do the right thing." Then you can say, "If I can show you a way to handle the situation more peacefully, so that you deal with it in a way that is more correct than an angry quarrel, would you be willing to try what I suggest?" Very likely the answer will be, "Yes."

*After hearing about the technique of asking someone for the main factor behind his position and then asking him the question, "If I can show you a better way...?" I tried it out on someone with whom I found it difficult to get along. I was hoping that this would be helpful. But to my surprise, the person just got angry at me.*

*"Why are you angry?" I asked him.*

"Because you are just using a technique, and I want you to be real," he replied.

"If you felt that I was sincere in wanting us to get along and that I would try to resolve the real issues that you were concerned about, would you be willing to explore the matter?"

"If that's what you would be really doing, then I'm willing to try," he said.

I saw that with a variation of the approach, I was able to make more progress than previously.

# 64

# YOUR THOUGHTS
# ARE ENERGY

E VERY THOUGHT YOU THINK IS ENERGY. WHETHER YOU create positive energy or negative energy all depends on the specific thoughts you think. For many people this awareness gives them more understanding of the power they have to create their reality.

The essence of all matter is energy. When this energy is released, it has tremendous power. If it is focused and channeled, it can supply a large amount of positive energy that serves as fuel for technological benefits. If, however, the energy explodes in a destructive way, it has the capacity to destroy what has taken years to build. On a smaller scale, each of us creates or destroys ourselves and our lives with the energy we create with our thoughts.

The thoughts you think about events and situations create the energy you experience from them. Critical, condemnatory, resentful, indignant, offended, aggrieved, and angry thoughts create negative energy in yourself. This leads to quarrels and arguments with others. Then they experience negative energy. Then you experience more negative energy because of the way they respond and the way you think about their response. Since you create this, you can choose to think calm, peaceful thoughts, and elevated, spiritual thoughts. These create positive, healthy energy in yourself. And then you are more likely to say things that will create positive energy in the mind of the other person.

Develop the habit of asking about your thoughts: "What kind of energy are these thoughts creating?" If positive, keep it up. If negative, choose more positive thoughts that very moment. Don't even have negative thoughts about your negative energy. You can tell yourself, "How grateful I am that I can choose positive energy producing thoughts right now."

*"I can't stand all these people who quarrel all the time," the peace lover said. "They give off such negative energy. It's awful the way they fight and argue so much. Just thinking about this makes me mad. Wherever you go, you find that people are quarreling. I even have dreams about the negativity of quarrels. I don't quarrel with quarrelsome people, I just avoid them like the plague."*

*I tried to point out as gently as I could that repeating these types of thoughts creates negative energy. At first the person kept arguing that anyone who loves peace will condemn quarrels.*

*"I suggest that you sing the praises of peace," I suggested. "This will create positive energy for yourself and might have a positive influence on some people."*

*The smile on this person's face showed that the message was received.*

# 65

# MISTAKEN ASSUMPTIONS

**M**ANY QUARRELS ARE CAUSED BY MISTAKEN assumptions. Person X thinks that person Y said or did something that person X did not say or do. Or person Y heard person X say something and he misunderstood his intentions and therefore was offended. If person Y would have understood person X's true intentions, he wouldn't have felt offended at all.

It's easy to say, "Let's not make any more mistaken assumptions." On the practical level, however, this is problematic. No one purposely wants to make a mistaken assumption. Whenever anyone makes a mistaken assumption, he doesn't realize that he is assuming wrongly. If he were to realize that this was a mistaken assumption, he would no longer make that assumption. The problem is that people don't even realize that they are assuming anything. They think that they are dealing with accurate facts, not mistakes.

Has anyone ever made a mistaken assumption about you? If so, you know what it feels like. Have you ever assumed something and then found out that the reality was different than what you have assumed? If yes, then you know that not all your assumptions are correct. Have you ever been a witness to someone else's mistaken assumption about another person? If yes, then you know that this can happen even to highly intelligent people.

Before quarreling with another person ask yourself, "How do I know for certain that I'm not making any mistaken assumptions?" Since you can't be absolutely certain, leave a little mental room open for updating and clarifying reality.

People who know how easy it is to make mistakes about what really was said and what was meant, about what really was done and why, are usually more emotionally centered. This enables them to speak up in a calmer tone of voice and with wording that leads to a more peaceful interaction.

*Many years ago I was involved in a situation where two sides were in an intense conflict with each other. Because I was younger, I didn't realize how easy it was for basically honest and intelligent people to make serious mistakes about the reality of a situation. Statements that had no basis in reality were made as if they were absolute facts. Each side assumed that the other side had malicious intentions. One side assumed that all the members of the other side were lying, while the other side assumed that their counterparts were mean-spirited and wild. By trying to find out what the truth actually was and by doing all the research possible, I found that people took statements out of context and therefore had totally distorted pictures. People took minor details and blew them up, and certain assumptions were made that had absolutely no basis in reality. In the heat of the quarrel, both sides felt so much animosity against each other, that they wrongly assumed negativity that was groundless.*

*Ever since then I have been much more careful about not assuming that I really know what anyone else has said and done. This has saved me from being involved in a number of heated disputes. And when I have been involved, I try to differentiate between what actually was known to have been said and done and what was merely assumed.*

# 66

# TRANSCENDING INSULTS

NSULTS ARE A PRIME CAUSE OF QUARRELS. INSULTS ADD FUEL to a quarrel. Insults can be remembered for a long time. To live a joyful, serene life, it is wise to learn to transcend insults. It is wise to learn to let insults go. And it is wise to refrain from repeating the insults of others to ourselves. The distress of an insult will only last for a few moments if your mind moves on to think of wiser and better things.

Insulting another person is a violation of a Torah commandment. Therefore we need to be as careful as possible never to insult another person. At the same time, we need to learn to view the insulting words of another person as "just words."

Some of the attitudes that will help us let go of insults are:

"My emotional state is based on the thoughts that I think. I will choose to think the thoughts most conducive to my total well-being. I will focus on the kind and compassionate things that have been said to me. I choose not to focus on anyone else's negativity."

"If there is any truth to the insult that this person said, I will learn from it. This person could have chosen a more pleasant, tactful way of making his statement. If he hasn't yet mastered a sensitive way of speaking, I hope he will, but I'm not going to allow myself to focus on his pattern of communicating."

"The insults should teach me to speak to others in ways that are respectful and kind."

"Life is too short to waste on being upset about the way that others speak. If I can point out to him that he should speak in a more refined and dignified way, I will point this out. Even if he won't listen to me or I feel that I can't point this out, I will spend my time thinking and acting in ways that enhance my life."

"Even though I did find his words distressful, I'm not going to cause myself more distress by repeating those words to myself over and over again. I will choose better things to repeat to myself."

"Gaining mastery over my emotional states makes me emotionally independent. This, too, will help me gain greater emotional independence."

"My goal is to not allow others to control my feelings with the way they speak. How this person chooses to speak is his choice. I am the only one who will decide how I would like to feel at a given moment."

"I will speak to this person with respect and I hope that this will influence him to reciprocate and speak to me with respect."

"My value was given to me by the Creator. No human being can take away even one tiny drop from that value."

A frequently asked question is, "Are you claiming it's easy to transcend insults?" Not in the least. It is a skill that takes thought and effort. But the benefits of transcending insults are that you make your emotional well-being independent of the refinement of character or lack thereof of any other human being. It is well worth striving for this goal.

*I was angry at someone who told me, "It's not that person's insults that are causing you so much emotional pain. It is your own attitude towards them. You are really causing yourself the emotional pain. So stop blaming others for the way they speak to you. You can't change the way anyone else speaks to you, but you can change the way you speak to yourself."*

*"It's not the way that I speak to myself that's the problem," I said angrily. "I have a sensitive nature and therefore I get hurt easily."*

*"Don't blame your nature. Become more aware of the way that you speak to yourself, and stop speaking to yourself in a way that increases the pain. When you are calmer about insults, you will find more effective ways of influencing people to speak more respectfully towards you."*

*I didn't like the tone of voice that this person used to give me this message, but I had to admit that he was correct. I would counterproductively repeat insults to myself over and over again. I would say to myself, "How dare he speak to me like that?" "It's awful that he's speaking to me this way." "I can't stand it when I am insulted."*

*I decided that one of my important goals would be to allow myself to rise above any insulting words of others. I would consistently speak to others with respect, and that itself is elevating. And*

I would tell others with respectful assertiveness that I would appreciate it very much if they would speak to me with respect.

The first person I said this to was the person who told me that I shouldn't take insults so personally. "What you said to me was correct and I needed to hear it. However, in the future I would appreciate it greatly if you would speak to me more gently."

I felt great when this person said to me, "I thank you for pointing this out. I'll be more careful in the future."

# 67

# WHAT DO YOU
# CHOOSE TO OVERLOOK?

QUARRELS COME FROM FOCUSING ON WHAT YOU don't like about someone. Peace comes from focusing on what you do like.

Each person has virtues and faults. When you keep your focus on someone's virtues, you feel more positively towards him. When you remember the positive things that this person has done for you, your gratitude will influence the way you speak and act. Focusing on virtues and gratitude makes it easier to overlook the mistakes and faults of another person. If you have positive ways of influencing that person, great! But that will be in the background, not the foreground.

Quarrels, resentment, and animosity all come from focusing on what you don't like, and overlooking this person's good and positive words and actions.

We all have a limited ability to keep information in the forefront of our consciousness at any given moment. Use this to help you feel more positively towards people.

"But if I don't remember the potential negative, I won't be in a position to protect myself," some will argue. "This person has hurt me in the past, so I have to remember to be careful in my interactions with him."

If someone is a great threat, like a terrorist or a cruel person, we definitely need to be on guard. The danger needs to be our main focus. But in the vast majority of instances, we are really safe. No one is suggesting that anyone get a lobotomy and totally erase the memories that remind you to be careful. Of course, you need to protect your well-being. But by focusing on a regular person's positive qualities, you are more likely to speak and act towards him in ways that reinforce those positively qualities. That person will usually feel more positively towards you, and this is likely to bring out the best in that person.

*A father who had difficulties with one of his children consulted an expert. "This child gets on my nerves. He speaks to me so insolently that invariably I get angry and we quarrel."*

*"Overlook the insolence," the father was told. "Speak to him the way you would if he were totally respectful. If your way of dealing with this in the past would have worked, you wouldn't be having a problem with this issue in the present. You tried different forms of criticism and rebuke. Since that didn't work, use your power of imagination to imagine that your child is speaking and acting like a model child. Your acting like a model parent is more likely to make your mental vision a reality. Be patient. The effects of this method can take time. As you are patient, you are serving as a role model for your son to be more patient also."*

# 68

# IT'S THE PRINCIPLE

*"I can't give in. It's not because I don't want peace. It's the principle of the matter."*

*"My ego isn't involved at all. I have to teach this person a lesson."*

*"For my sake, I would just let it go. But if I don't put my foot down, this person won't treat others with respect."*

*"I have a principle. I don't forgive someone unless he apologizes in a formal matter. Just saying, 'I'm sorry,' isn't sufficient for me."*

PRINCIPLES AND VALUES ARE VERY IMPORTANT. BUT THE principle of "Loving peace and pursuing peace," is a higher principle than most. At times, our *yetzer hara* (evil inclination) appears in the form of righteousness. We might claim our ego isn't involved. We need to teach someone a lesson. But if someone didn't speak to us with respect or didn't treat us in the way we want to be treated, we can assume that our ego is involved.

We might have a true dilemma: "What is the right thing for me to do in this particular instance? Objectively speaking, should I give in or not? Should I forgive or not?" Then we should consult a Torah scholar to clarify the right thing for us to do. An objective wise person will give us a more accurate distinction between what is really principle and what is really ego.

When in doubt: Go for peace! There is a higher probability that the principle of peace will elevate you.

*I met an elderly, joyful person who consistently ignored slights and avoided petty arguments.*

*"It's not right for others to treat you without the highest respect," someone said to him. "Why don't you stand up for the principle that you should be treated with respect?"*

*"My most important principle is that I should treat other people with respect. I hope that others will learn from my example. Another principle is that I want to live a joyful life. Demanding that others treat me with respect won't really get me true respect, but it will actually cause me distress, and a lack of joy. I prefer to work on real principles and not on ego masquerading as principles."*

# 69

# IF I GIVE IN,
# HE WILL FEEL THAT
# HE WAS TOTALLY RIGHT

SOME PEOPLE ARE AFRAID TO GIVE IN ON SOME RELATIVELY minor things that will create peace. "If I give in, the other person will feel that he is totally right," is the essence of what they say.

Let's analyze this. First of all: What will happen if you don't give in? It's highly unlikely that the person will then say, "Since this person didn't give in that means that I'm wrong and he's right." What usually happens is that the person thinks he's right and you're wrong, and that you are too stubborn to acknowledge it, or else your bias prevents you from seeing the truth that he is right and you are wrong. Since he will think this way whether or not you give in for the sake of peace, the question is, "Given that his opinion will be the same whether or not there is peace, is it preferable for me to make peace?"

Secondly, in the vast majority of quarrels, what is the actual loss to you if the person feels that you have acknowledged that he is right and you are wrong? It is different when practical financial issues are involved: Then you have to make financial calculations of advantages and disadvantages to decide on the wisest move. But when nothing practical is lost by his thinking that he is right, you don't have a real loss. "It's an unpleasant feeling," one could respond. That's probably true, but you can change this for yourself by feeling the joy of doing what it takes for the sake of peace. This will put you in a positive state and raise your self-image.

*When I was a child, during a ball game at recess I gave in to a classmate's arguments that he scored a point, which I felt he didn't really do. I felt it was an unpleasant waste of our recess time to keep on arguing over something that didn't make a real difference.*

*But this fellow kept taunting me, "See. Now even you admit that I was right. Come on. Tell everyone how you were wrong and I knew better than you. I'm always more accurate."*

*This infuriated me. My sense of justice was aroused. His reaction was blatantly unjust. This memory kept coming back to me whenever I was about to give in during an argument. Looking back, I realize I really lost a lot because of this childhood experience.*

*After I was married, my refusal to given in caused much marital strife. In a conversation I had with a rabbi I was told, "The sign of a person with a great self-image and authentic inner strength is the ability to quit an argument without having to prove to anyone else that he was right." That broke the spell of my childhood experience. I now felt empowered by ending quarrels, regardless of what the other person might mistakenly think.*

# 70
# FINANCIAL DISPUTES

THE TALMUD (*EIRUVIN* 65B) STATES THAT ONE OF THE KEY factors that reveal who we really are is the way we deal with money. Money plays a major role in everyone's life. Having it, not having it, losing it, trying to gain it, trying to protect it, spending it, not spending it, sharing it with others, accomplishing with it, risking it, and the list goes on and on. Money can play a central role in arguments, quarrels, and feuds.

Remaining calm about money matters can be a challenge. But being nervous, worried, stressed out, and irritable about money won't make someone wealthy, nor will it prevent poverty.

Mastering the ability to be calm in reference to money will prevent quarrels over insignificant amounts. Some people fight over literally pennies, and their arguments cost them a much greater loss than they gain.

Discuss your financial disagreements calmly. You might have to be persistent; if so, be calmly persistent. When you negotiate, negotiate calmly. And even with major financial disagreements, you will be much better off not saying or doing anything that will needlessly create a bitter quarrel.

The more someone loves peace, the more open he will be to forego money that would necessitate involvement in a quarrel.

Loving peace doesn't mean that one needs to lose out financially. But in many situations, by foregoing relatively minor sums one will gain much inner peace. The benefits to one's spirituality, health, and emotions will be worth more than the money involved.

How much money are you willing to spend to do a *mitzvah* (good deed)? Many people joyfully spend large sums for charity and for other good deeds. How much money are you willing to spend to avoid a quarrel? This will reveal a lot about your character.

*"I was overwhelmed and furious," someone shared with me. "I was being sued over something that wasn't at all my fault. I felt like calling up the individual who was suing me and verbally blasting him. Fortunately, I contacted a competent lawyer.*

*"'Cool it,' my lawyer told me. 'Stay calm. Don't call up the lawyer who sent you the letter, and don't contact the fellow who is suing you. I'll take care of it. I feel almost certain that when I send this fellow's lawyer my letter, he won't continue the suit. And if he does take it to court, I'll handle it. I'm absolutely positive that in court, you'll win. He doesn't really have a case against you.'*

*"I was grateful for his advice. Getting emotionally charged by a potential financial loss prevents clear thinking. Saying the wrong thing always make things worse."*

# 71
# IMPULSIVITY

WHEN IN THE MIDST OF A QUARREL, IT IS EASY TO react impulsively. Your first thoughts might not be in your best interests. So patiently wait and think. Weigh your various options. Even when you think carefully about the wisest course of words and actions, it's still possible to make mistakes. But reacting impulsively will make mistakes much more likely.

Some people wait for a long time to take action. But then they feel they have waited long enough and take action impulsively anyway. At each stage of action, weigh the pros and cons of the next step. Even if at first the action you were planning seemed the best thing to do, after taking a few steps you might reconsider and choose to refrain from continuing that course of action. Always think as clearly as you can. Always take the entire picture into consideration.

Some people aren't impulsive in action, but they are impulsive with their thinking. They make up their minds about a situation right away, and regardless of what else they hear, their minds are closed. Part of being patient is to be patient and open with your thinking. Whether you're involved in a quarrel yourself, or just listening to a situation that is being described by the parties involved, don't jump to conclusions. Wait until you get the fullest picture possible before you make your decisions.

*At the funeral of the late Rabbi Yisroel Gustman, who was a rabbinical judge in Vilna prior to World War Two and head of the Netzach Yisroel Yeshiva in New York and later in Jerusalem, his son-in-law related how Rabbi Gustman had a tremendous understanding of people. When people spoke to him about a quarrel, he would listen patiently for a long time. Then he would tell the people to return the next day. The next day, he asked them to relate all the details of the situation. When the long session finished, he asked them to return the next day. On the third day, Rabbi Gustman once again asked questions to clarify the details of the story. He had the people repeat everything they had to say once more. They assumed that the elderly Rabbi hadn't remembered everything they said and needed to hear the story again to refresh his memory. But soon they saw how mistaken they were.*

*After hearing the entire story for the third time, Rabbi Gustman would point out how the order of what they said changed each time they repeated the story. The emphasis was different in the various accounts. From hearing all three versions, Rabbi Gustman was able to clarify the total picture. This took intelligence and memory, insightful understanding, and patience. Those who are inclined to react impulsively, would be wise to remember this.*

# 72

# THE MEMORY OF THE WRITTEN WORD

**M**EMORY IS FRAGILE. MEMORY IS EASILY DISTORTED because of bias and self-interest. Memory is subjective. Frequently we remember the way we remember because we want the situation to be favorable to us. We are referring to the memory of a person who is honest and truthful. All the more so, the memory of someone for whom truth is not a priority.

When you write down facts and agreements, you can look them up again to refresh your memory. It's amazing what some written words can do for you.

The saintly Chofetz Chaim, who was a paragon of virtue and elevated character, always insisted that every agreement he made with someone be written down. He loved peace and didn't want to become involved in a needless argument or quarrel. So whenever a situation would arise where differences in memory could cause a problem, he would gently insist that all the details of every agreement be written on paper and signed by both parties.

Wasn't he afraid that asking the other person to write down their agreement and sign it was sort of making a statement that he didn't trust the other person? He was much more afraid of the negativity and harm of a quarrel. Perhaps he would forget some details. Perhaps the other person would forget some details. If you are dealing with someone who is truly dishonest, a written agreement might not be worth the paper it was written on. But even honest people make honest mistakes. We can't prevent all of them; but whatever we can prevent, we should.

*A friend of mine made a complex financial deal with someone and told the other person that he wants to write the final agreements on paper for them to sign.*

*"What's the matter with you?" the would-be-partner shouted at him. "Don't you trust me? Don't you think that I'm honest? You are guilty of suspecting an innocent person. This is an insult of the highest order. I refuse to write down anything. I trust you and I want you to trust me."*

*My friend responded, "I definitely don't mean to insult you. But for me it's a prerequisite to write down all agreements. If we don't write it down, I'm afraid that I can't go through with the deal."*

*The deal fell through. Not long afterwards, my friend became aware that someone else had made a deal with the would-be-partner and was intimidated by this person's attacking him when he suggested they write down the agreement. The person made the deal without signing and then had a long, drawn out court battle to get his money back from his dishonest partner.*

## 73
# MOCKING REMARKS

REFRAIN FROM MAKING MOCKING REMARKS. WHEN ANGRY at someone, many are tempted to utter or mutter insults. Hold on. What you don't say won't cause you harm or loss. What you don't say won't prolong the quarrel. What you don't say won't cause bitterness and animosity. And what you don't say won't boomerang and come back to strike you.

Quarrels are caused by insults and are prolonged by insults. The Torah prohibition against insulting other people is called *onoas dvorim*. In a previous book, *The Power of Words*, I have elaborated on details and specific examples. The general principle is: Any words that cause someone pain or anguish is considered a violation of this prohibition.

Insults beget insults. When you insult someone, that person is likely to insult you back. And then you are likely to insult that person back. The dueling interchange often produces only losers and no winners.

When two people insult each other, each one usually has a better memory of the insults that the other person said. Therefore when they talk about this to others, or even when reviewing it in their own minds, they focus on the painful, mean, and nasty things that the other person said to them.

They conveniently forget the painful, mean, and nasty things that they said. And if they do remember what they themselves have said, they often justify it as, "I only said this or that, which isn't that bad. What this person said to me was much worse than what I said to him." The ironic thing is that both parties think these same thoughts, which means that they both feel that the wrong they did was minimal, while the wrong of the other person was much greater.

If you insulted another person, you owe him an apology. Even if that person did insult you also, your insulting him wasn't the best thing you could have done. The ideal is to master the ability to remain calm and clear thinking when someone insults you, and to only say words that will improve the situation. Often the wisest thing is to say nothing. The general rule is to think before you speak, and ask yourself, "What can I say right now that will be beneficial?"

*I met a person who worked on insults. He used to think that it made him look intelligent to put others down with witty put-downs. If he ever heard a "clever" insult, he made an effort to remember it and to look for an opportunity to use it. He enjoyed insulting people before others who would admire his humor, wit, and intelligence. He was under the impression that they thought highly of him. I told him, "You might think that people admire and respect you because they smile at your witticisms at the expense of others. You are mistaken. Deep down they look at you as a mean person with an inflated ego. Some people are intimidated by you;*

*they don't want to be victims of your sharp tongue. If you knew how much damage you are causing yourself, you would resist the temptation to use your power of speech as a sword."*

*At first he argued with me. When I saw that I couldn't convince him, I told him that at least he should keep an open mind to the possibility that what I told him was valid. About two months later he came back to me and said, "I recently wanted to be elected for an honorary position. I thought that certainly most of the people who knew me would vote for me. But the person who ran against me won by a landslide. I know that I am more appropriate for that position. I guess what you told me was right. I am now committed to being more careful with how I speak to others."*

## 74

# SELF-DECEPTION ABOUT ONE'S MOTIVES

IT'S EASY FOR A PERSON WHO IS INVOLVED IN A QUARREL OR fight with someone else to claim that his motives are only the highest, the best, and the most elevated. But ego, hurt feelings, greed, or envy are often the real motives behind the quarrel. At times the easiest person to deceive is oneself.

Some participants in a quarrel will say things like:

"I'm doing this because it's the right thing to do, not because of selfish reasons."

"I can't condone this person's wrong. That's my real reason for this quarrel."

"If I let this person think he can say or do anything he wants, he will continue to do this. So this quarrel is really for his ultimate benefit."

"I'm not involved in this quarrel for personal gain. I want to help others."

A paradigm of this is the Torah's account of Korach's rebellion against the great leader Moses. Korach claimed that every single individual was holy. Why then did Moses take leadership for himself and make his older brother Aaron the High Priest?

The Sages teach that Korach's true motivation was envy (see Rashi's commentary to *Numbers* 16:1).

Whenever ego, hurt feelings, greed, or envy could be a basic root of why one is involved in a specific quarrel, one needs to be totally honest with oneself. "Why am I really involved in this quarrel?" we need to ask ourselves.

It's very easy to claim motivations that sound good to others. But when we are by ourselves and all is quiet, we need to introspect. We need to ask ourselves for our true reasons. It takes tremendous courage to acknowledge to ourselves that we are motivated by less than lofty reasons.

Having the courage to realize that we are motivated by base motives can motivate us to interact more peacefully: We no longer are adding the strength of idealism and elevated values to the fire of our battle.

*I asked a brilliant Torah scholar what he would suggest to do in a specific situation where two members of the same family were quarreling. I didn't mention any details at all as to the identity of the people involved. Nevertheless, he immediately said, "Regardless of the claims of the people involved, envy is most likely the root cause. Take a look at the* Book of Genesis *and you will find that the root of family feuds is usually envy." Knowing this won't automatically solve the quarrel. But at least it's a step forward in understanding the underlying issues.*

# 75

# BEING RIGHT, DEAD RIGHT

IN COURSES ON SAFE DRIVING, THERE IS A SLOGAN, "YOU might be right, dead right. But it's better to be safe and healthy." You might have the law on your side. What you want to do is technically correct and proper. But if you are dealing with someone who is going against the light or stop sign, you would be wise not to claim your rights. Focus on being safe and healthy and make your decisions accordingly.

The same principle applies to getting into quarrels. If you are dealing with someone who is rational, reasonable, and wants to do the right thing, you might be able to discuss your disagreements calmly and sensibly. The other person might see that you are right and he will totally concede to your arguments. Even if you both continue to disagree, he might be willing to make a relatively fair compromise that is basically win-win. But if you are dealing with someone who is tough and mean and nasty and dishonest, along with some other negative characteristics, be smart.

What does it mean to be smart? That, of course, will depend on the uniqueness of each situation. Weigh the pros and cons of every option you can consider: What are the advantages of this option? And what are the disadvantages? When the advantages of one option minus its disadvantages are greater than that of other options, that might be the option to choose. Keep in mind that the definition of advantages and disadvantages is subjective: It all depends on what you personally feel you will experience.

*I had to make a decision: Should I take my adversary to court? A number of my friends kept insisting that I go forward and battle the issue in court. "It's totally clear that you are right," they said. But someone who knew me well said, "It could be that you have right on your side. But the other person is so tough and unscrupulous that what you will lose out by trying to claim your rights will make this move a total mistake. You're better off spending your time and energy on alternative ways to make money."*

*Having had a number of unpleasant experiences when I felt that I was right and seeing that being right didn't automatically mean that everyone who was involved would see it my way, gave me the inner strength to forego a potential gain to avoid an almost certain heavy loss. Looking back later, I was glad that I made this decision.*

# 76
# MISREPRESENTING YOUR POSITION

MANY PEOPLE FIND IT IRRITATING, AT TIMES intensely so, when the other party in an argument misrepresents their position. Some people might purposely try to ridicule what you have said by claiming that you said something absurd, which you definitely didn't say or mean. Other people, or the same people at other times, truly misunderstand your position. What they say you said is not at all what you said, but they think it is.

Don't let this pattern throw you. Don't let it get you off-balance. Stay calm. Stay centered. And even if you are seething inside, don't say anything that will escalate the quarrel. Be prepared for times like this. Some statements you can practice making until they become automatic include:

"I don't blame you for getting upset about what you think I meant. But that wasn't my intention at all. I would like to explain what I said in different words, so I will make myself clearer."

"I would like to clarify what I actually said."

"This is a misrepresentation of my position."

At times you might ask an adversary, "Did you do that on purpose?" The reply usually will be, "Do what on purpose?" And you can reply, "Misstate my position." The other party will say, "Of course I didn't purposely misstate your position." Then the person may apologize for misrepresenting your position. This is the preferred reaction. Or the person will argue that you really said and meant what he said you did. Then it's usually best for you to respond calmly, "In my mind I said such and such. I apologize to you for not saying it the way I thought I did."

If being misquoted pushes your buttons, use every instance of being misquoted as an opportunity to master remaining calm, patient, centered, focused, and flowing, regardless of what another person says.

*I noticed that when someone would say that I thought or felt a certain way that I didn't think or feel, I would raise my voice in irritation.*

*"Why does this bother me so much?" I asked myself. Contemplating this, I realized that it came from a need to avoid disapproval from others. I didn't want anyone to think that I wasn't as intelligent, insightful, perceptive, aware, or discerning as I saw myself. The solution then would be to increase my level of emotional independence. I needed to overcome the need for approval. Moreover, by explaining my position as clearly as possible in a calm, peaceful way I had a better chance of showing the other person what I really thought or felt.*

# 77

# "JUST DO IT MY WAY."

*"We don't need to argue and quarrel about so many things. Just do everything the way that I want, and we will have peace."*

THERE IS SOME TRUTH TO THIS STATEMENT. YES, IF ONE person does everything exactly the way the other person wants things to be done, and doesn't do anything that the other person doesn't want him to do, they won't argue and quarrel. But to an objective reader it seems like an unfair demand, doesn't it?

You, the reader, might find yourself on either side of this statement. Perhaps you might be someone who makes this statement. You blame the other person for any arguments and quarrels. If he wouldn't be so insistent on having things his way, you would all get along peacefully. Neither of you would get angry and you would both be speaking pleasantly to each other.

Unless you are a total tyrant and dictator with a powerful police force to back you up, it's unlikely that you will consistently find people who are willing to go along with your attitude. Not everyone will be willing to do everything exactly the way you want. So if you want to get along harmoniously with others, you need to learn to make fair compromises at times.

If you are on the receiving end of this philosophy, it can make life difficult if the other person is older, or bigger, or tougher, or an authority with whom you need to interact regularly. Each situation is unique, and the wisest thing to say and do depends greatly on the total picture of the entire situation.

A general piece of advice is the words of the Sages (*Tomid* 32), "Who is wise? The person who thinks about the outcomes." Avoid needless clashes with someone who espouses this "do it my way" attitude. Think of ways that you can work around it quietly and gently, and you will often be able to do things the way that you would wish if you don't directly confront that authoritarian personality.

The best solution would be to motivate that person to become more humble and more open to allowing you to do things differently. However, people with this attitude are not usually highly flexible, and are likely to resist change. But who knows? Perhaps if you pray well and try wisely, you can make enough progress to improve the quality of your relationship with this person.

*Someone who used to demand that everything always be his way related, "I ran a successful company. I demanded that everyone who worked for me do things the way that I wanted, whether they liked it or not. I paid my employees well, and those who didn't want to abide by my policies were welcome to look for another job.*

"My first three marriages didn't work out. I was considering marrying for the fourth time, and my potential wife said to me, 'I respect the strength of your character and your consistency. But when you interact with me, I need more flexibility. I want us to discuss matters and to work out solutions that are mutually acceptable. If you agree to this, we'll get married. If not, forget it.'

"I appreciated the inner strength of this person, and I knew that I would lose her unless I would treat her as an individual with a unique personality and with ideas that would differ from my own. I carefully weighed the pros and cons and concluded that I would be better off marrying her and giving up the need to be totally in control. It took a lot of effort on my part to follow through on my agreement, but I knew that my life would be so much better if I made this difficult change.

"Looking back, I realize that I had lost out a lot by making unreasonable demands on others, and now I have a much more balanced approach, even in my business."

# 78

# DON'T BE
# BULLIED MENTALLY

SOME PEOPLE WHO QUARREL WITH YOU MIGHT BE BULLIES. These are people who want their way without any concern, care, or sensitivity for the needs of others. They might shout and scream. They might use crude or subtle insults and putdowns. They will persist and obstinately demand that you give in to their requests. They tend to aggressively use the power of intimidation. Some bullies might even have an outward showing of being polite, but they don't reason with you and negotiate. Rather, they try to push you into going along with what they want.

What goes on within your mind is up to you. Never be bullied mentally. Depending on the circumstances, at times it's wiser to give in rather than fight, and at times it's wiser to take a stand. But regardless of what you feel the situation calls for on the behavioral level, inwardly increase your inner strength and sense of empowerment. Your value is a given, and nothing this person says can take away from that intrinsic infinite value.

Mentally move back. You might want to imagine that person on a screen or stage in front of you while you are sitting far away, observing him at a safe distance. You might want to imagine that you are outside in a car and you are sending in an actor who is playing the role of a psychiatrist. Psychiatrists frequently need to interact with people who have dysfunctional and angry personalities, but they don't take it personally. All the more so, an actor who is playing the role of a psychiatrist. All the more so when you leave your consciousness, as it were, in a car outside, away from the interaction. This gives you greater mental freedom.

Those who become intimidated easily might find it helpful to visualize the bully as a tiny baby wailing for what it wants. Or to imagine that the bully is really a robot. This evens out the playing field and can protect someone from feeling needlessly overwhelmed.

Stay centered, focused, and flowing the entire time. The more negative this person is, the less you should take what he says seriously. His mode of communication reflects his present character. Eventually, he may refine his character and elevate the way he speaks. Your character is based on the way *you* speak and the way *you* act. And by mentally staying in a centered, focused, and flowing state, you will have a greater ability to speak and act in wiser ways.

*"Up until I was in my mid-thirties I didn't get into many quarrels,"* this gentle middle-aged man related. *"But I did go around with a distressed feeling that I was giving in too much. I was intimidated when people threatened to get angry. I gave in*

when people raised their voices or had an angry look on their faces. I was overly concerned about what people would think of me. And this made it easy for bullies to cause me financial losses. My self-image was knocked, and I felt that it was impossible for me to stick up for myself.

"Then I read a book that told me that I had a right to ask for fair treatment. I had a right to not give in to anyone who tried to intimidate me through anger. As long as I was not actually in danger of physical harm, the fact that someone was much bigger and stronger and had a much more powerful voice was not a reason that I should give in to anything that I thought wasn't fair. Over time, I realized that having a sense of empowerment and inner strength is a state that I can keep on developing throughout my life. I have mastered the ability to be gently assertive. I say, 'No,' when I need to say, 'No.' I am persistent about getting my point across. I have learned from experience that as long as I am firmly outspoken, I don't need to raise my voice or say anything that is insulting. I engage in discussions that I previously might have viewed as quarrels, but now I realize that protecting myself from being bullied is not a lack of peace."

# 79

# SKEPTICS, CYNICS, AND SARCASM

THERE ARE CERTAIN PATTERNS THAT OTHERS MIGHT USE that could arouse your anger and start or prolong quarrels. If you use these patterns you might get others angry. If it's not your intention to provoke a quarrel, it's valuable to be aware of these patterns and choose other patterns that are more respectful.

Some people view the statements and actions of others with skepticism and cynicism. At times they may be right, but often they are wrong. Moreover, others might have mixed motives. They might have positive intentions, and yes, self-interest does play a role.

If you have positive intentions for your words and actions, don't allow someone's negativity to upset you. The key is to remain calm. Getting angry at someone who challenges your motivations doesn't prove to him that you have the most elevated motivations. Protesting too much is often a sign that there is at least a kernel of truth in what the other person has said. It really could be that you protest because the other person's cynicism is way off the mark, but that's not what a cynic thinks. From his point of view, the calmer you remain, the more your counter-statements will be respected.

A sarcastic way of speaking can be infuriating. And that's exactly the intention of the person who uses it: He is trying to get you angry. He can try, but only you can help him succeed. Don't. Calmly respond to a sarcastic remark, "I would appreciate it if you would speak in ways that are mutually respectful." If the person is usually reasonable, you might say, "I find sarcasm irritating. I would appreciate straight statements, so we can discuss the issues." In extreme situations, you might challenge a person who is consistently sarcastic, "Why do you feel a need to use sarcasm?" But this is likely to get the other person angry at you. With a chronic offender, you might feel it's worthwhile trying this, but be prepared for a sarcastic remark.

And what about the possibility of your speaking sarcastically to others? Since you wouldn't like it if others spoke to you sarcastically, don't do unto others what you would not want them to do to you.

*When I was in school, there was a classmate who would frequently say, "Oh, sure." This bothered me. I approached him with a request that he stop saying this. I began by saying, "I would like to get along well with you," and of course, he immediately said, "Oh, sure." After each sentence I said, he would repeat these two words. I felt like punching him, but controlled myself. Instead I said to him, "Just think of how you would feel if someone constantly said this to you whenever you tried to speak to him. Realize that you cause others to dislike you. For your own good, make the intelligent move and stop saying this." He once again said, "Oh, sure." Then I said to him with intensity, "Please stop saying this." He could tell from my tone of voice and the look on my face that I was totally serious. I didn't raise my voice and I didn't threaten in any way, but I wasn't going to tolerate this.*

*The next day he came over to me and actually thanked me for being so strong. "I realize that I shouldn't be doing this, but it became such a strong habit that I found it difficult to stop. I really appreciate your getting your point across."*

# 80

# CHARMING IN FRONT OF OTHERS

SOME INDIVIDUALS CHOOSE TO BE CHARMING, POLITE, and pleasant in the presence of certain people, when they feel they will benefit by acting this way. But with others, they are argumentative, biting, angry, and aggressive.

If you are on the short side of this, you know how frustrating it is. You see the negative aspects of this person and are highly distressed by the patterns of what he says and how he says it. But if you approach people to help you out, they say things like, "This person is so charming, it must be totally your fault." "This person is so polite, it must be totally your fault." "This person is so pleasant, it must be totally your fault." Not only are you not being helped, you are also being blamed entirely for a situation that, at least in part, is caused by the other person's patterns.

If you find yourself in such a situation, be mentally prepared to deal with it. Otherwise, you might be thrown off balance. If you speak to some authority or expert who will be trying to make peace, focus on your goal. Your goal shouldn't be to condemn the other party and try to convince others that that person is much worse than they seem now. Rather, focus on your goal, which is to motivate this person to act in his charming, polite, and pleasant way towards you.

When speaking to the person himself, it's best to say, "I appreciate how positive, charming, polite, and pleasant you are many times. I would greatly appreciate it if you would be like this more often when you and I interact." It's important to say this in a tone of voice that is mutually respectful.

If you are trying to make peace between two people and one or both are presently charming, polite, and pleasant, and one or both people say, "In front of you the person speaks and acts this way, but with me he is angry and aggressive," realize that the reason you are involved is exactly because this person acts positively in some contexts and not in others. Therefore, your goal is to motivate and influence this individual to be charming, polite, and pleasant with the person in whose presence he isn't yet this way.

Some people, who are often charming, polite, and pleasant with others but not with the person to whom you are now speaking, might say, "It's entirely this person's fault. Ask anyone. I am always charming, polite, and pleasant. So if I'm not this way with this person, it proves it's all this person's fault." What you want to convey is, "It's great that you are charming, polite, and pleasant with so many people. And your goal should be to be this way with this person also. Which patterns would you like this person to upgrade, so that you can both interact in a way that's mutually satisfactory?"

*I was involved in a distressful interaction that served as an eye-opener for me. There was a person who pushed my buttons the wrong way. I blamed him for it. I would say, "I don't have to change anything. I'm friendly and cheerful with the vast majority of people. It's entirely this person's fault."*

*We went to speak to a rabbi who we felt could help the situation. I began by repeating the above statement, which I had been repeating many times in my own mind. And then the other person said the exact same thing that I did! He also claimed to be friendly and cheerful with others and therefore, it was all my fault.*

*The rabbi smiled and said, "You both are friendly and cheerful when you speak with me. Let's see what we can do to take that as our model and goal. Just as you are this way towards me, let's see how to master speaking this way with each other."*

*I realized that the other person was just as right, or wrong, as I was. We both needed to learn to speak and act at our best with each other.*

# 81
# DON'T FALL INTO A NAÏVE TRAP

SOME SCHEMING MANIPULATORS MIGHT TRY TO UTILIZE a peacemaker's good intentions to negotiate a better deal than is really fair. They will search for someone who will influence their adversary to "give in for the sake of peace."

Some people who owe others money might try to find someone to convince the lender to forget about collecting the money, for the sake of peace. Or someone might know that if he goes to court, he will have to accept a deal that is not as favorable to him as he thinks is possible. He will therefore involve a peacemaker. In order to speed up the process, the peacemaker might pressure the more easy-going person to agree to a deal that is clearly unfair to those who are experienced in these matters.

Awareness of the possibility of this pattern will help you avoid it. Each situation is unique, and what is necessary is a comprehensive view of the entire situation.

Even knowing this, at times it's worthwhile to agree to a negotiated deal that is basically one-sided. If one party has strongly negative character traits and is potentially dangerous, it might be wiser to accept the least of the potential evils. This is a pragmatic calculation and the one who decides if it's worthwhile should be the individual who will be affected by the decision. If you feel it's worthwhile for him, you can clearly tell him so, but as long as he is mentally competent, let him decide.

*I had to work together with a professional mediator on an especially difficult and complex situation. One party was highly irrational and had an awful temper. Dealing with him was fraught with danger.*

*The mediator finally got the irrational person to agree with something. The minor concession took a lot of time and effort. The mediator told the victim, "In a regular situation I wouldn't tell anyone to agree with this. But in our situation, it's best for you to agree and move along with your life." The individual followed the mediator's advice and agreed that accepting it was the smartest thing to do. One needs to know when to cut one's losses.*

# 82

# Don't Make
# Things Worse

WHEN PEOPLE TELL YOU STORIES ABOUT WHAT someone else said or did that they didn't like, what you say can make things better or worse. At best, think about what you can say to improve matters. Even if you can't improve a situation, be careful not to make things worse.

Some people mean well. They are very empathic. When they hear that someone said something insulting, they react with statements such as, "You poor thing. That was awful of him to say that to you. He's a rotten person." Or they might say, "If anyone ever said anything like that to me, it would mean a fight. I never let anyone get away with saying anything like that. The next time you see that person, insult him back. Tell him off as strongly as you can." While the intentions behind these type of statements might come from a place of caring for the feelings of the person who was insulted, the contents of these statements are likely to inflame a quarrel.

Some people enjoy making things worse. They like the drama and excitement of "a good fight." They might feel a sense of power if they can say things that will arouse your anger at another person. They might be envious of the other person or dislike them for their personal reasons, and they might say things that will cause a fight that wasn't there before, or make an existing quarrel more intense. If someone ever tries to do this to you, don't fall into the trap of the *yetzer hara* (evil inclination).

*A rabbi who has a lot of experience with making peace between people told me, "Well-meaning relatives and friends often say things that cause a bigger problem than was there before they spoke up. Whenever there is a quarrel, every move either brings the two people closer to a resolution or further away from one. Condemning the other person as being an evil, totally insensitive, and uncaring individual is often incorrect as far as the facts go. Strategically, while trying to improve the situation they themselves are causing their friend or relative more pain, rather then truly helping. With the vast majority of people, when both sides see each other in a basically positive light, they can work things out, even though the other person has said and done things that they shouldn't have. I have at times approached people whom I feel have made things worse and told them my thoughts on the matter. Reactions have varied, but the ones who are the most sincere about truly helping people are open to learn from the feedback, and even appreciate hearing how they themselves can improve what they do."*

# 83

# WITHSTANDING NEGATIVE APPROACHES OF OTHERS

W HEN YOU HAVE A CONFLICT WITH ANOTHER person, the comments from other people will either help you move towards resolution and peace or send you in the opposite direction.

Some people will encourage you to see the positive in the other person, to speak positively, and to work out the conflict in ways that are win-win, or at least close to this.

But there are other people who, for various reasons, will say things to you that will make you even angrier at the other person. They will try to provoke you to escalate your conflict and quarrel.

Some of the things they might say are:

"Don't allow yourself to be a doormat. Scream and shout and say all that is on your mind."

"Only by expressing your anger at its fullest will the other person see the light and act positively towards you."

"Force and aggression are the only things this person understands."

"It's awful that he insulted you like that. Tell him off, he deserves it."

In extreme situations, the only thing that will protect a person is counterforce. But this is the exception, not the norm. With the vast majority of people, staying calm, centered, and focused, and speaking reasonably, will accomplish more in more productive ways.

Don't let the negativity of others become yours. Find positive ways to defend your rights and work out peaceful solutions at the same time.

*I tend to see the good in people and it's a high priority for me to get along peacefully with others. I would prefer to give in to others for the sake of peace. For me this isn't being passive, but it's an active decision to pay a reasonable price for peace. I am willing to do what's necessary to defend myself, but in most instances my wisest moves are the peaceful moves.*

*I was once involved in a quarrel with someone over large sums of money. I was told by a few people, "The only way to handle this is to be more aggressive than the other person." I bought into their way of looking at things. The distress and aggravation that this caused me was intense. Not only did I end up suffering myself, my family members also became involved, and the situation kept escalating.*

*I now realize that there is no such thing as, "The only way to handle this is..." Whoever says this isn't aware of the full range of multiple possibilities. Looking back, I can see that if I would have been true to my own nature and attitudes, I would have handled the conflict in ways that would have been much more peaceful. It's too late for me to turn back the clock, but from now on I am dedicated not to allow the negative comments of those who mean well to prevent me from finding peaceful solutions.*

## 84

# DON'T JUDGE OTHERS

THE MORE YOU VALUE PEACE, THE MORE CAREFUL YOU must be not to judge others who lack peace. If you're not involved, it's easy to say, "Why don't they just make peace?" "Why don't they get along better?" "They should interact with smooth harmony. I don't see why they don't."

People might not be able to work together because of ideological differences. Each person might each see the other as dangerous to his own well-being; interacting with the other person is highly stressful. Two people might have such diverse personalities and priorities that it's almost impossible for them to do things together.

When two people or two parties don't get along, they might have a distressful history of which you are unaware and which they don't feel like sharing with others.

The Sages teach, "Don't judge another person until you reach his place." If you were in his exact place, you might have spoken or acted the exact same way he did. Perhaps better, but perhaps worse. Since you can't know exactly what he has experienced, any judgment on your part would be missing important factors that could change the meaning of why someone is speaking and acting the way he is.

I've met peace advocates who have made me a bit wary of those who are excessively exuberant about pursuing peace. These peace advocates are highly judgmental of others who don't pursue peace the way these people think they should. Their approach is much too aggressive for my tastes. And then I realize that I am guilty of being too judgmental towards them.

# 85

# FIND AN OBJECTIVE MEDIATOR

OBJECTIVE MEDIATORS MIGHT HELP YOU INTERACT better with someone with whom you find communication difficult. A competent mediator will be able to keep all parties in calmer states. A competent mediator will be able to clarify each person's position. A competent mediator will make editorial suggestions to delete inflammatory remarks and at times explain how to be clearer by being more concise. A competent mediator will be able to clarify misconceptions and errors.

In the presence of a third party both individuals agree to, they will usually be more reasonable. They will usually talk more respectfully, or at least more calmly. And if emotions do flare up, by listening and understanding the mediator creates a more constructive atmosphere.

Mediators can differ in their approach. Some are more authoritative and might tell one side they are right and the other side that they are wrong. When both sides accept the authority of the person they consult, they will resolve the issues between them. Other mediators view their mandate more as a coach than a judge. They coach both sides so that a working relationship is created for the mutual benefit of both sides. If you feel that you can benefit from a mediator, find someone whose approach and style is acceptable to everyone involved.

*In our company we had a group of strong personalities. We felt that if everyone would work together we would accomplish much more than we did. But the situation was absolutely outrageous. The sense of competition among our employees brought out a tough and aggressive side that was intolerable if we wanted to succeed at the level we felt we could.*

*We called in a professional mediator to meet with our staff, but the situation didn't improve. Over time, we held meetings with a number of mediators. The situation eventually improved a bit, but after time the old patterns resurfaced.*

*"I guess it's impossible for us to work in harmony," said an outspoken member, and the others nodded their heads in agreement.*

*But the head of our department didn't give up. He met a mediator at a conference and was impressed by what this person had to say. He invited him to speak to our company. This mediator had a strong belief in the essential goodness of people. We all felt that he was impartial and fair. He showed us patterns that he felt would work for us. They did and we've all benefited.*

# 86
## "He Agreed with Me."

When two people or two sides have an argument or quarrel, what often happens is the following: One person will tell his side of the story to a friend, an expert, or a major scholar. Based on the version he told the friend, the expert, or the scholar, he was told something to the effect of, "Well, I don't know the entire picture, but according to what you told me, you are right."

Then this person will tell the other party, "I discussed this with others and they agreed that I am right. I was objective, and told all the facts of the situation the way they actually happened."

Now the other person might relate his side of the story to a friend, an expert, or an authority, and the response might be something similar to, "The other person isn't here to tell me his version, but if what you say is accurate, it seems as if you are right."

And then when the two parties report with glee that their friends, experts, and scholars agree with their position, they both stick to their original positions. Sometimes they both will say, "Well your friend, expert, and scholar didn't hear my side of the situation from me directly. And now that you told them your side and they made up their minds, they are biased towards what you told them, so I don't think that I will get a fair and objective hearing."

There is a Torah law that forbids a judge to listen to one litigant if the other litigant isn't present. When only one party is there, details that would make a difference could be left out. Someone can even purposely leave out some factors that would present his case in an unfavorable light. Even if one party feels that every last detail was told, this is usually an impossibility. In every interaction between two people there are a multitude of factors and it's inevitable that not every detail will be conveyed. Also, people tend to remember what the other person said that would have been better not said, and they tend to forget what they said that would have been better not said.

If you and another person would truly like to know the real opinion of a third party about the disagreement, you both need to speak to that third party at the same time the first time you describe the situation.

People who are consulted about a disagreement by only one party should realize that even if they aren't officially judges and don't mean to render a legal decision, they are not getting a total picture of what happened. They should be very careful to qualify their remarks and say, "Without hearing both sides, I don't know the entire picture." They should also realize that even when they say, "I'm not saying this as a final opinion, but based on what I hear now you are right," they are likely to be quoted as, "He told me that I was right." Somehow the qualification gets lost.

*I once tried to explain my side of an argument to a major scholar with much life experience. I described the situation in as much detail as possible and tried to be as objective as I possibly could. "Do you think I am right?" I asked.*

*"I don't know," replied the scholar.*

*"But I just gave a picture of the entire situation," I said.*

*"Yes, but since the other person didn't give me his view, I don't know."*

*I kept asking for a tentative opinion, but he adamantly refused to give an authoritative statement. When I walked away, I felt frustrated. I felt that he certainly had an opinion on the matter; why was he afraid to state it? Then when I cooled down, I realized that he was right. He hadn't heard the other side. If he were to have tentatively stated an opinion, I might have quoted him as agreeing with me. And with his experience, he must have had many instances when hearing the other side of the story gave an entirely different meaning to the facts.*

# 87

# TIME RELEASE SUGGESTIONS

THERE IS A STRONG TENDENCY TO WANT IMMEDIATE results. We might try to influence two people to make peace with each other, but may not feel that anything we said made any difference. We might be wrong. There is a possibility that we were more successful than we thought we were.

Some suggestions take time to have a positive effect. We might tell two relatives or two erstwhile friends how they will benefit by resolving their quarrel. We might describe how they both will gain from making peace. They might tell us why they can't possibly have peace. They might tell us they tried and nothing worked. They might both tell us that the other person's way of speaking makes it impossible for them to get along. But later on they might think about what we said and be motivated to try once more. Eventually they might find ways to get along peacefully.

Describe the benefits of making peace as vividly as you can. After suggestions about how they can speak in mutually respectful ways, make suggestions about how they can put each other in positive states. Suggest that they spend some time thinking this over.

You might say, "Picture how wonderful it will be when you have peace. When you are calm and relaxed, spend some time visualizing it. Be on the lookout for positive ways to speak that will create peace. Maybe you will dream a dream that will give you insight into how to get along better with this person. Perhaps you will read something that will motivate you to make an all-out effort to make peace. Let what I'm telling you be stored in your brain. Let the ideas be repeated over and over again. With enough repetitions, you will intensify your feelings that peace is so important, that you will do everything you can to make peace. Feel the great feelings that you will feel when you successfully create a peaceful relationship."

*I spoke to someone who spends a lot of time trying to make peace between people engaged in quarrels. "Don't you become discouraged when you see that you've spent a lot of time with people and didn't make progress?" I asked him.*

*"I never know for certain that I didn't make progress," he said. "I had many experiences when I spoke to people for a long time and they didn't seem to budge at all. But after days, weeks, and even months, they reported back to me that what I had told them had a positive effect. At first they didn't think that anything I said would make a difference, but they eventually saw that the ideas I had suggested came popping up in their minds. I usually add sentences suggesting that what I've said to them will go with them, and they themselves might be surprised to see that they will speak and act in ways conducive to peace."*

# 88

# CAN NOTHING
# BE DONE?

THERE ARE DIFFICULT AND COMPLEX QUARRELS ABOUT which it is easy to think, "Nothing can be done to resolve this." But the reality is that as long as both parties are alive, there is always a possibility that something might work.

You and people you consulted might say, "There is nothing possible to do." It is impossible for any single human being to know all the possibilities, regardless of how great, wise, and creative that person is. There might still be something that could work.

Even the most stubborn human being might change his mind. Even if he won't "change his mind," he might make a new decision. Please note this last sentence because it's very valuable when it comes to making peace. People can always look at a situation differently than they did before. The way they saw it before, they were unwilling to make peace. But now new factors have developed, and because of these new factors they will agree to make peace: Now they might see you in a more positive way. Now they might have upgraded their character traits and you might have upgraded your character traits.

Now you might judge each other more favorably. Now you are both more committed and determined than ever before to make peace.

In the field of getting people to change the way they are thinking and the way they are acting, there exists an unlimited number of clever and ingenious possibilities. At times someone with not that much experience and not that much wisdom will still be able to come up with an approach that will work.

So in certain situations you might decide that since no one has found a practical solution until now, there might be better ways to utilize one's time. Also, the negativity of the quarrel while it is still raging can be so problematic that it isn't spiritually, physically, and emotionally healthy to be involved with the other party of the quarrel. But still be aware that a resolution still might be found. Just knowing that a resolution can be found will help you think in that direction.

*I knew a couple who quarreled and fought from even before they were actually married. For years they argued and spoke about divorce. They had gone to a number of professional counselors and all sorts of advisers, but nothing worked. Some things did help for a week or two, but nothing made a lasting difference. There were told over and over again, "Nothing will work for you."*

*I bumped into the husband after not seeing him for a long time. He was all smiles. He told me, "I thought that we'd never have a peaceful relationship. Nothing we did seemed to work. Then when we both decided to seek a divorce, we said to one anoth-*

er, 'Since we're ready to give up anyway, let's choose to enjoy each other's company until we get divorced.' And somehow that worked for us. We canceled our plans for the divorce and it's amazing how wonderfully well we get along now. I can't really tell you anything specific that worked for us. It was that new choice we made that somehow brought out the best in both of us."

# 89

# KNOW YOUR
# LIMITATIONS

THE MORE IDEALISTIC YOU ARE, THE MORE YOU MIGHT FEEL that you should make peace whenever you hear that two people are quarreling. Sometimes, you will be able to make the right suggestions to encourage peace and to help those quarreling overcome the obstacles to peace. But at other times, even though you might mean well, you will be limited in your ability to help. Knowing your limitations will enable you to focus on what you *can* do, and not expend your inner resources in ways that will frustrate you and could even make a quarrel worse than it was before.

Sometimes the only way that you will find your limitations is by trial and error. Please note the possibility that even though you might think that nothing you say will be beneficial, at times what you say will be very helpful. Even when you aren't able to create a total resolution of the quarrel, you might be able to influence both sides to speak with greater mutual respect. The more experience you have, the more you will know your strengths and weaknesses. Someone with little experience might not even realize that he will be clueless about what needs to be said and done to improve a situation. And someone with little experience might be so optimistic about being able to help that he actually will be helpful.

In some situations the parties will only listen to someone whom they both accept as an authoritative expert. And in other situations they'll only listen to someone who is a close friend of both parties. In other situations someone who is a close friend to one party will be able to tell that party, "I've always been your friend and I still am. And I'm telling you that what you are saying and doing isn't right. You need to apologize."

Many limitations are temporary. We all lack knowledge when we are infants. Gaining knowledge is a lifetime process. The greater your understanding of the thoughts, feelings, and motivations of people and what is needed to influence them, the greater your success in helping people make peace. Keep upgrading your skills, and you will be able to accomplish more.

*I met someone who was highly successful in making peace between people even when many others had tried and had given up. I asked him what special knowledge and skills he had.*

*"The truth is that I don't have any special knowledge and skills," he said. "But it pains me deeply when people I know aren't getting along. I feel a profound and intense drive to influence both parties to make peace. I am willing to speak to people as long as it takes."*

"Do you think that some people who try to make peace aren't successful because they lack this sincerity and drive?"

"I don't feel qualified to make general comments about why some people aren't successful. But I do feel comfortable saying that having a strong inner drive to make peace helps a person overcome potential limitations."

# 90

# AT TIMES
# ONLY DISTANCE
# WILL PREVENT QUARRELS

OUR FOREFATHER ABRAHAM WAS THE EPITOME OF kindness and compassion. Even when he personally suffered, his focus was on helping total strangers. Nevertheless, we find in the Torah that he felt a need to keep a distance from his nephew, Lot.

Both Abraham and Lot had shepherds who worked for them. A quarrel broke out between the two groups of shepherds. Abraham told Lot that the quarrel of their shepherds was likely to lead to a quarrel between them. In order to avoid this, Abraham told Lot that they needed to move away from each other.

Abraham gave his nephew a choice. "You can travel to the right and I will travel to the left. Or you can choose the left and I will move to the right." Exactly because Abraham loved peace, he was aware of a potential challenge that was likely to be problematic.

We might find ourselves in frequent clashes with particular people. When this is the case, we should try to do all we can to get along harmoniously. If after repeated tries we see that nothing is working, it could be wiser to keep a distance. But don't act this way prematurely. When solutions can be found, even if they take time, search for those solutions.

And just as Abraham went to rescue Lot when he was captured, so too we should go out of our way to help someone even if we found that we weren't able to interact peacefully on a regular basis.

*"I was having a difficult time getting along with a roommate, and I consulted one of the rabbis in our yeshiva,"* an elderly person related about an incident in his youth.

*"'I would like to have this roommate moved out of my room,' I requested. 'I find it difficult to get along with him.'*

*"'Who says that he should leave? Abraham gave Lot a choice. Perhaps you should be the one who finds another room. But before we take drastic action, let's see if we can find a way for you two to get along. Never be impulsive about deciding that you absolutely can't get along with someone,' was my rabbi's advice.*

*"My rabbi gave me a few helpful tips, and while we still didn't become the best of friends, we did get along peacefully."*

# 91

# PEACE AT ANY COST CAN BE TOO EXPENSIVE

ISN'T THERE A LIMIT TO WHAT ONE SHOULD PAY FOR PEACE? The answer is: Yes. There is a time for peace and a time for war. Defending oneself is a valid right. Passively losing everything isn't wise.

So the question arises: What are the guidelines to know when we should make sacrifices for peace and when not? The answer is beyond the scope of this book and beyond the competence of the author. Consult wise and elevated scholars for specific situations. Unfortunately, many hot-tempered or mean-spirited people decide relatively easily and quickly that a situation calls for an aggressive battle.

Gandhi's peaceful resistance worked because his opponent was Great Britain, which had values that precluded an all-out, unlimited military response. When one deals with a ruthless enemy, one needs to select approaches that are appropriate for the needs of the situation.

In day-to-day, more common situations, the price of peace isn't usually that costly. The expense of quarrels and feuds is often much greater.

"I'm going to fight this person in court, no matter how much the legal battles will cost me. I'm willing to pay a fortune not to let this person think that he is right and I am wrong."

The lawyer this person consulted was an experienced, calm, and clear thinker. He was a man of integrity and advised the angry potential client, "If you insist on going to court, and you want me to represent you, I will. But if you want my honest opinion, I'm advising you to save your money. The amount of time, energy, and money that this legal battle will cost you isn't worth it. Even if you end up winning in court, the price will be too high. My experience is that some people in similar situations take my advice and later on are glad that they did. Those who persist and battle it out, are usually sorry. The ones who are mean-spirited might feel in the end that even though they did lose out a lot, it was still worth it. The perverse pleasure of causing the other person distress and a loss of money was what they wanted more than personal gain. You seem to me to be more idealistic than that. I'd rather earn my living as a lawyer dealing with cases that are more worthwhile."

The individual who told me this story relates that he followed the lawyer's advice. Looking back he has no regrets.

# 92
# TIME IS RUNNING OUT

W E ALL HAVE LIMITED TIME ON THIS PLANET. WE have a mission to complete, whether or not we are clear about its exact nature. Time is life, and life is the most precious thing we have.

Each time we speak, we answer the question, "How will I spend the precious time that I have left?" With each action we take, we answer the same question. Time wasted on fruitless quarrels is time we don't have enough of to waste. This time consists not only of the amount of time we actually engage in a specific quarrel, but also the time one spends thinking and even obsessing about it.

We never know how much precious time we have left. Compared to eternity, no matter how long the amount, it is microscopically brief. We can do much good in this world. We can spend our time wisely elevating ourselves. Isn't it unwise to spend time lowering ourselves? Even when you have conflicting of ideas, interests, or opinions, maintain your own and the other person's dignity and then the time spent will be qualitatively different. This will allow you to discuss issues in an atmosphere more conducive to efficiency.

Cherish each moment of life. And when you do, you will find it much easier to refrain from saying things that would possibly prolong a quarrel. You will find it much easier not to say or do things that could create a quarrel in the first place. And you will have the strength to take the initiative to end a quarrel even if it means apologizing first when you would prefer that the other party be the first one to do so.

Peace enables you to make the most optimal use of your valuable time. Becoming aware of the specific time at any given moment can always serve as a reminder, "It's time for peace."

*I met someone who avoided quarrels like a plague. He never responded to insults or slights to his honor. He gave in when he could have stood his ground and argued. He refused to talk about any unpleasantness between himself and anyone else, unless it would be to resolve a specific issue. Then he was totally open to discussing an issue as long as it would take.*

*"Why is it so important to you not to be involved in quarrels?" he was asked.*

*"My beloved Creator gave me the gift of life. For how long, I won't know until the end. When I am asked how I spent the time of my life, I want to have a good answer. I certainly don't want to respond that I wasted this gift by saying and doing things that were disrespectful to another person."*

# 93
# BELIEVE IN MIRACLES

"IT WILL TAKE A MIRACLE FOR THESE TWO PEOPLE TO GET along well."

It might take a miracle. And miracles happen each and every day. Life itself is a miracle. Your breathing is a miracle. Your brain and its ability to read are miracles. Every time you stand up and walk you are experiencing a miracle. Every time you talk and listen you are experiencing a miracle. Every time you eat and your body digests food and sends nutrients to each and every cell is a miracle.

It might take a miracle for a person who frequently becomes angry to conquer his anger. And this miracle can happen. The more you believe in the possibility of this miracle, the more likely it is to happen.

It might take a miracle for a given individual to stop insulting you and putting you down. And this miracle can happen.

It might take a miracle for this person to think sensibly and reasonably. And this miracle can happen.

There are miracles in everyone's life. Some people recognize this more than others. By recognizing the miracles in your life, your entire experience in this world is on a higher plane. And when it comes to believing in the miracle of getting along better with someone with whom you find it difficult to get along, looking for miracles might bring about what is commonly called a self-fulfilling prophecy. This makes it easier for you to assume that other quarrels might be resolved in ways that at first didn't seem likely.

*As an exercise, it was suggested that I write a list of at least thirty miracles that happened to me or to people I've met. If I couldn't think of so many at one sitting, I could keep adding to my list for the next thirty days. This opened my eyes to seeing things that I wouldn't otherwise have recognized as being so remarkable. A number of items on my list were improvements in the ways people acted.*

# NOTES

# NOTES

# NOTES

# NOTES

# NOTES

# NOTES

# NOTES

# NOTES

# NOTES

# NOTES

# Other Books
# by Rabbi Zelig Pliskin

 **Books**

---

**Courage**
**Enthusiasm**
**Happiness**
**Kindness**
**Patience**
**Serenity**

 **Books**

---

**Anger, The Inner Teacher**
**Marriage**
**My Father, My King**